THIS BOOK BELONGS TO

The Library of

....

....

Copyright @2023

All rights reserved. No part of this publication may be reproduced, stored in a retrieval system, or transmitted in any form or by any means, electronic, mechanical, photocopying, recording or otherwise, without the prior written permission of the Publisher.

I can't tell you how grateful I am that you decided to read my book. My most heartfelt thanks that you took time out of your life to choose my work and I hope you find benefit within these pages.

There are so many books available today that offer similar content so that makes it even more humbling that you decided to buying mine.

Tell me what you thought! I am eager to hear your opinion and ideas on what you read as are others who are looking for a good book to buy. Leave a review on Amazon.com so others can benefit from your wisdom!

With much thanks.

Table of Contents

What's the best way to read this book?	28
Getting started	38
Why the fear of starting?	39
Alone or with a co-founder?	41
Documenting everything to find the co-founder	49
Becoming a teacher	50
Key learnings	54
Idea	56
Stop looking for ideas - start looking for problems to solve	56
Service audience success	58
How to validate an idea quickly?	67
The art of bootstrapping	72
3 rules to live by as a bootstrapped entrepreneur	75
Key learnings	81
Build	83
Build something you want	83
The two types of MVPs	84
Getting your first customers	87
The launch booster - doing lifetime deals?	90
Key learnings	97
Grow	98
3 things we failed at that you should avoid	98
4 things we shouldn't have done that made us successful	104
Building a growth engine	114
Community first - Building in Public	139
Key learnings	150
Scale	152
Scaling your audience building	152
Together we're stronger	157
Build a family, not a community	167

No product, no money	171
Team is everything	172
Process rhymes with success	177
Be transparent	180
Getting media coverage	185
Key learnings	195
Exit	196
Why should you sell your SaaS company?	196
Why shouldn't you sell your company?	198
How much is your SaaS business worth?	199
How to find buyers for a SaaS product?	202
What are the different stages to go through until the sale?	204
4 things to avoid at all costs	210
The $150M valuation	211
Why Expedition Growth Capital?	215
Key learnings	219

SUMMARY

The Power of Financial Transformation refers to the significant impact and potential that financial changes and improvements can have on individuals, businesses, and even entire economies. It encompasses a wide range of strategies, practices, and initiatives aimed at enhancing financial systems, processes, and outcomes.

Financial transformation involves the adoption of innovative technologies, such as artificial intelligence, machine learning, and blockchain, to streamline and automate financial operations. These technologies enable faster and more accurate data analysis, improved risk management, and enhanced decision-making capabilities. By leveraging these tools, organizations can optimize their financial processes, reduce costs, and increase efficiency.

Furthermore, financial transformation involves the implementation of robust financial planning and analysis frameworks. This includes the development of comprehensive budgeting and forecasting models, as well as the establishment of key performance indicators (KPIs) to measure and monitor financial performance. By adopting these practices, businesses can gain better visibility into their financial health, identify areas for improvement, and make informed strategic decisions.

Financial transformation also encompasses the adoption of sustainable and responsible financial practices. This includes integrating environmental, social, and governance (ESG) factors into investment decisions, promoting transparency and accountability in financial reporting, and aligning financial strategies with long-term sustainability goals. By incorporating these practices, organizations can not only drive positive social and environmental impact but also enhance their reputation and attract socially conscious investors.

Moreover, financial transformation involves the development of financial literacy and inclusion initiatives. This includes providing individuals and communities with the knowledge and skills necessary to make informed financial decisions, access financial services, and build financial resilience. By empowering individuals with financial literacy, societies can reduce poverty, promote economic growth, and foster social stability.

The power of financial transformation is evident in its ability to drive economic growth and development. By improving financial systems and processes, organizations can attract investment, stimulate entrepreneurship, and create job opportunities. Additionally, financial transformation can enhance financial stability, reduce systemic risks, and promote financial inclusion, thereby contributing to overall economic resilience and sustainability.

In conclusion, the power of financial transformation lies in its ability to revolutionize financial systems, processes, and outcomes. By leveraging innovative technologies, implementing robust financial planning and analysis frameworks, adopting sustainable practices, and promoting financial literacy and inclusion, organizations can unlock significant benefits and drive positive change. Whether at an individual, organizational, or societal level, financial transformation has the potential to shape a more prosperous and sustainable future.

The Intriguing $150 Million Secret is a captivating and mysterious story that revolves around a hidden fortune worth a staggering $150 million. This secret, shrouded in secrecy and intrigue, has captured the attention of many individuals, sparking curiosity and speculation about its origins and the identity of its rightful owner.

The story begins with a chance discovery made by a young archaeologist named Emily, who stumbles upon a hidden compartment in an ancient artifact during an excavation in a remote archaeological site. Inside this compartment, she finds a cryptic message that hints at the existence of a hidden treasure worth an astonishing $150 million.

As news of this discovery spreads, a wave of excitement and anticipation sweeps across the globe. People from all walks of life, including treasure hunters, historians, and even ordinary individuals, become consumed by the allure of this secret fortune. The media frenzy surrounding the story only adds fuel to the fire, as everyone becomes eager to uncover the truth behind this enigmatic secret.

As the search for the rightful owner of the $150 million treasure intensifies, a series of clues and riddles emerge, leading the treasure hunters on a thrilling and perilous journey. The clues take them to various locations around the world, each holding its own set of challenges and obstacles. From ancient ruins to hidden caves, the treasure hunters must navigate through treacherous terrain and solve intricate puzzles to unlock the next clue.

Along the way, the treasure hunters encounter a diverse cast of characters, each with their own motivations and agendas. Some are driven by greed and the desire for personal gain, while others are driven by a sense of justice and the need to return the fortune to its rightful owner. Betrayal, alliances, and unexpected twists add layers of complexity to the story, keeping readers on the edge of their seats.

As the treasure hunters inch closer to unraveling the mystery, they begin to uncover a web of deceit and corruption that spans generations. The $150 million secret is revealed to be more than just a hidden fortune; it holds the key to a long-buried family secret, a scandal that could shake the foundations of society.

In the final climactic moments, the treasure hunters must confront their own demons and make difficult choices that will determine the fate of the $150 million secret. Will they be able to overcome the challenges and uncover the truth? And what will happen once the secret is finally revealed?

The $1000 investment is a financial decision that involves allocating a specific amount of money towards an investment opportunity with the expectation of generating a return or profit. This investment can take various forms, such as stocks, bonds, mutual funds, real estate, or even starting a small business.

When considering the $1000 investment, it is important to evaluate the potential risks and rewards associated with different investment options. This involves conducting thorough research and analysis to identify investment opportunities that align with one's financial goals, risk tolerance, and time horizon.

One possible investment option for the $1000 could be investing in stocks. Stocks represent ownership in a company and can be purchased through a brokerage account. With $1000, an investor can buy shares of one or multiple companies, depending on the stock prices. It is crucial to research and select companies that have a strong track record, solid financials, and growth potential. Additionally, diversifying the investment by investing in different sectors or industries can help mitigate risk.

Another option for the $1000 investment is investing in bonds. Bonds are debt instruments issued by governments or corporations to raise capital. By purchasing bonds, investors essentially lend money to the issuer in exchange for regular interest payments and the return of the principal amount at maturity. Bonds are generally considered less risky than stocks, but they also offer lower potential returns. It is important to assess the creditworthiness of the issuer and the prevailing interest rates before investing in bonds.

Mutual funds can also be a suitable investment option for the $1000. Mutual funds pool money from multiple investors to invest in a diversified portfolio of stocks, bonds, or other assets. This allows investors to access professional management and diversification, even with a relatively small investment amount. It is crucial to carefully review the fund's investment strategy, performance history, fees, and expenses before investing in a mutual fund.

Real estate can be another avenue for the $1000 investment. While $1000 may not be sufficient to directly purchase a property, it can be used as a down payment for a real estate investment trust (REIT) or a real estate crowdfunding platform. REITs are companies that own, operate, or finance income-generating real estate properties. Investing in a REIT allows individuals to indirectly invest in real estate and potentially earn rental income and capital appreciation. Real estate crowdfunding platforms, on the other hand, allow investors to pool their funds with others to invest in specific real estate projects.

The concept and ideation phase is a crucial step in the development of any project or product. It is during this phase that ideas are generated, refined, and evaluated to determine their feasibility and potential for success.

The first step in the concept and ideation phase is to clearly define the problem or need that the project or product aims to address. This involves conducting thorough research and analysis to understand the target audience, market trends, and existing solutions. By gaining a deep understanding of the problem, the project team can identify opportunities for innovation and develop unique ideas that will set their product apart from competitors.

Once the problem is defined, the next step is to generate ideas. This can be done through brainstorming sessions, individual creativity exercises, or by seeking inspiration from other industries or domains. The goal is to generate a wide range of ideas, regardless of their feasibility or practicality at this stage. Quantity is key during this phase, as it allows for a diverse pool of ideas to choose from.

After the ideation phase, the project team must evaluate and refine the ideas generated. This involves assessing each idea against a set of criteria, such as market potential, technical feasibility, and alignment with the project's goals and objectives. Ideas that do not meet these criteria are discarded, while those that show promise are further developed and refined.

During the concept development stage, the selected ideas are transformed into tangible concepts. This involves creating prototypes, sketches, or mock-ups to visualize and communicate the proposed solution. These concepts are then presented to stakeholders, such as investors, clients, or end-users, for feedback and validation.

The concept and ideation phase is an iterative process, meaning that ideas are continuously refined and improved based on feedback and new insights. This allows for a more robust and well-rounded concept to emerge, increasing the chances of success in the later stages of development.

In conclusion, the concept and ideation phase is a critical step in the development of any project or product. It involves defining the problem, generating a wide range of ideas, evaluating and refining those ideas, and transforming them into tangible concepts. This phase sets the foundation for the rest of the development process and greatly influences the ultimate success of the project or product.

Building hype and anticipation is a strategic approach used by businesses and individuals to generate excitement and interest around a product, event, or upcoming release. It involves creating a buzz and generating curiosity among the target audience, ultimately leading to increased engagement and sales.

One of the key elements in building hype and anticipation is effective marketing and promotion. This can be achieved through various channels such as social media, email marketing, influencer collaborations, and traditional advertising. By strategically planning and executing these marketing efforts, businesses can create a sense of anticipation and generate excitement among their target audience.

Creating a teaser campaign is another effective way to build hype and anticipation. This involves releasing small snippets or hints about the upcoming product or event, without revealing too much information. Teasers can be in the form of short videos, cryptic messages, or sneak peeks, which leave the audience wanting more. This approach creates a sense of curiosity and anticipation, as people eagerly await the full reveal.

Utilizing influencers and brand ambassadors can also play a significant role in building hype and anticipation. These individuals have a strong following and influence over their audience, making them ideal partners for generating excitement. By collaborating with influencers, businesses can leverage their reach and credibility to create buzz around their product or event. This can be done through sponsored content, giveaways, or exclusive access, which further fuels anticipation among the audience.

Another effective strategy is to create a sense of exclusivity. By offering limited edition products, early access, or VIP experiences, businesses can make their audience feel special and privileged. This exclusivity creates a sense of urgency and desire, as people strive to be part of the select few who have access to the product or event. This approach not only builds hype and anticipation but also drives sales and creates a loyal customer base.

Engaging with the audience and creating interactive experiences can also contribute to building hype and anticipation. This can be done through contests, challenges, or interactive social media campaigns. By involving the audience in the process, businesses can create a sense of ownership and excitement, as people eagerly participate and await the outcome. This approach not only generates buzz but also fosters a sense of community and connection with the brand.

In conclusion, building hype and anticipation is a strategic approach that involves effective marketing, teaser campaigns, influencer collaborations, exclusivity, and interactive experiences. By implementing these strategies, businesses and individuals can generate excitement and interest around their product, event, or upcoming release.

Immediate Reactions and Early Reviews provide valuable insights and feedback on a particular product, service, or event shortly after its release or debut. These initial responses are often shared by consumers, critics, or industry experts who have had the opportunity to experience or witness the offering firsthand.

When it comes to products, immediate reactions and early reviews can shed light on various aspects such as the quality, functionality, design, and overall user experience. Consumers who have purchased or used the product can provide feedback on its performance, durability, ease of use, and any potential issues or shortcomings they may have encountered. This feedback can be crucial for both the manufacturer and potential buyers, as it helps identify areas for improvement and informs purchasing decisions.

Similarly, early reviews of services can offer valuable insights into the level of customer satisfaction, the efficiency of the service delivery, and the overall value provided. Customers who have utilized a particular service can share their experiences, highlighting the strengths and weaknesses of the service provider. This feedback can be instrumental in shaping the service provider's future offerings and improving customer satisfaction.

In the case of events, immediate reactions and early reviews can provide a glimpse into the overall success and impact of the occasion. Attendees and participants can share their thoughts on various aspects such as the organization, venue, program, speakers, and overall atmosphere. This feedback can help event organizers gauge the effectiveness of their planning and execution, identify areas for improvement, and make necessary adjustments for future events.

Immediate reactions and early reviews are not only beneficial for consumers and users but also for the creators, manufacturers, or organizers. They provide an opportunity for continuous improvement and refinement of offerings, ensuring that they meet the needs and expectations of the target audience. Additionally, these initial responses can generate buzz and influence the perception of the product, service, or event among potential customers or attendees.

In conclusion, immediate reactions and early reviews play a crucial role in shaping the success and development of a product, service, or event. They provide valuable feedback, insights, and recommendations that can guide future improvements and inform purchasing decisions. Therefore, it is essential for both consumers and creators to actively engage in sharing and analyzing these initial responses to foster growth and enhance the overall experience.

Managing rapid success can be both exciting and challenging. When a company experiences rapid success, it means that it is growing at an accelerated pace and achieving its goals at a faster rate than anticipated.

While this may seem like a dream come true for many businesses, it also brings with it a unique set of challenges that need to be effectively managed.

One of the key challenges of managing rapid success is ensuring that the company's infrastructure and resources can keep up with the increased demand. This includes having the right systems and processes in place to handle the increased workload, as well as ensuring that there is enough manpower to meet the growing demands of the business. It may be necessary to hire additional staff, invest in new technology, or expand the physical space to accommodate the increased production or service delivery.

Another challenge is maintaining the quality of products or services during periods of rapid growth. As the company expands and scales up its operations, there is a risk of compromising on quality in order to meet the increased demand. It is important for management to prioritize quality control and ensure that the company's standards are upheld, even in the face of rapid growth. This may involve implementing stricter quality control measures, providing additional training to employees, or reevaluating suppliers and partners to ensure they can meet the increased demand without compromising on quality.

Additionally, managing rapid success requires effective communication and coordination within the organization. As the company grows, it becomes more important than ever to ensure that everyone is on the same page and working towards the same goals. This may involve implementing regular team meetings, setting clear expectations and goals, and fostering a culture of open communication and collaboration. It is also important to ensure that employees feel supported and empowered to handle the increased workload and responsibilities that come with rapid success.

Furthermore, managing rapid success requires a strategic approach to decision-making. With rapid growth comes a multitude of opportunities and choices, and it is crucial for management to make informed decisions that align with the company's long-term vision and goals. This may involve conducting thorough market research, analyzing data and trends, and seeking input from key stakeholders. It is important to strike a balance between seizing opportunities for growth and ensuring that the company's resources are allocated effectively and efficiently.

In conclusion, managing rapid success is a complex task that requires careful planning, effective communication, and strategic decision-making. While it can be an exciting time for a company, it is important to address the challenges that come with rapid growth in order to sustain long-term success.

Tracking sales and revenue is a crucial aspect of any business. It involves monitoring and recording all the transactions related to the sale of products or services and the corresponding revenue generated from these sales. This process provides valuable insights into the financial performance of a company and helps in making informed business decisions.

To effectively track sales and revenue, businesses employ various methods and tools. One common approach is to use a sales tracking system or software that allows for the systematic recording and analysis of sales data. This software typically includes features such as inventory management, order processing, and customer relationship management, which help streamline the sales process and ensure accurate tracking of sales and revenue.

The sales tracking system enables businesses to monitor sales activities at different levels, such as individual sales representatives, teams, or regions. This allows for better performance evaluation and identification of areas that require improvement. By tracking sales and revenue, businesses can identify their top-performing products or services, as well as the ones that are underperforming. This information can be used to optimize marketing strategies, adjust pricing, or make necessary changes to the product or service offerings.

In addition to tracking sales, monitoring revenue is equally important. Revenue tracking involves keeping a record of all the income generated from sales, including both cash and credit transactions. This information helps businesses understand their cash flow and profitability. By analyzing revenue data, businesses can identify trends, such as seasonal fluctuations or changes in customer preferences, and adjust their strategies accordingly.

Tracking sales and revenue also plays a crucial role in financial reporting and forecasting. Accurate and up-to-date sales and revenue data are essential for preparing financial statements, such as income statements and balance sheets. These statements provide a snapshot of a company's financial health and are used by stakeholders, such as investors and lenders, to assess its performance and make investment decisions. Furthermore, sales and revenue data are used in financial forecasting to project future sales and revenue figures, which are essential for budgeting and planning purposes.

Overall, tracking sales and revenue is a fundamental practice for any business. It provides valuable insights into the financial performance of a company, helps in making informed business decisions, and ensures accurate financial reporting and forecasting. By implementing effective sales tracking systems and analyzing sales and revenue data, businesses can optimize their operations, improve profitability, and stay ahead of the competition.

The key takeaways from the journey can be summarized as follows:

1. Self-discovery: Throughout the journey, individuals often experience moments of self-discovery. They learn more about their strengths, weaknesses, and capabilities. This self-awareness helps them make better decisions and navigate through challenges more effectively.

2. Resilience: Journeys are often filled with obstacles and setbacks. However, individuals who embark on these journeys develop resilience. They learn to bounce back from failures, adapt to unexpected situations, and persevere in the face of adversity.

3. Growth: Journeys provide ample opportunities for personal and professional growth. Individuals learn new skills, gain knowledge, and expand their horizons. This growth not only enhances their capabilities but also opens doors to new opportunities and experiences.

4. Perspective: Journeys offer a fresh perspective on life. By stepping out of their comfort zones and immersing themselves in new environments, individuals gain a broader understanding of different cultures, beliefs, and ways of life. This expanded perspective fosters empathy, tolerance, and a deeper appreciation for diversity.

5. Goal-setting: Journeys often involve setting goals and working towards achieving them. This process of goal-setting helps individuals clarify

their aspirations, prioritize their actions, and stay focused. It also instills a sense of purpose and motivation, driving them towards success.

6. Independence: Journeys encourage individuals to become more independent and self-reliant. They learn to make decisions, solve problems, and take responsibility for their actions. This newfound independence not only boosts their confidence but also equips them with essential life skills.

7. Connection: Journeys provide opportunities for individuals to connect with others. Whether it's meeting new people, forming friendships, or building professional networks, these connections enrich their lives and create lasting memories. They also foster collaboration, support, and a sense of belonging.

8. Reflection: Journeys often offer moments of reflection and introspection. Individuals have the chance to step back, evaluate their experiences, and learn from them. This reflection helps them gain insights, make adjustments, and grow as individuals.

9. Adaptability: Journeys require individuals to be adaptable and flexible. They encounter unfamiliar situations, navigate through different environments, and interact with diverse cultures. This adaptability not only

enhances their problem-solving skills but also prepares them to thrive in an ever-changing world.

Changing Lives with the $150m Secret is a groundbreaking initiative that aims to transform the lives of individuals and communities through the utilization of a $150 million fund. This fund, which remains undisclosed to the public, holds the key to unlocking a multitude of opportunities and possibilities for those who are fortunate enough to be a part of this life-changing program.

The initiative is designed to address various societal issues and challenges that individuals and communities face on a daily basis. It recognizes the importance of providing support and resources to those who are in need, and aims to empower them to overcome obstacles and achieve their full potential.

One of the key aspects of Changing Lives with the $150m Secret is its focus on education. The initiative recognizes that education is a powerful tool that can break the cycle of poverty and provide individuals with the skills and knowledge they need to succeed in life. Through the fund, scholarships, grants, and educational programs are provided to individuals who may not have had access to such opportunities otherwise. This enables them to pursue higher education, vocational training, or other forms of skill development, ultimately opening doors to better employment prospects and a brighter future.

In addition to education, the initiative also addresses healthcare and wellness. It recognizes that good health is essential for individuals to thrive and reach their full potential. Through the fund, individuals and communities are provided with access to quality healthcare services, including medical treatments, preventive care, and mental health support. This ensures that they can lead healthy and fulfilling lives, free from the burden of illness and disease.

Furthermore, Changing Lives with the $150m Secret recognizes the importance of economic empowerment. The initiative aims to create opportunities for individuals to become financially independent and self-sufficient. This is achieved through various means, such as providing microloans, business grants, and entrepreneurship training. By supporting individuals in starting their own businesses or expanding existing ones, the initiative not only helps them improve their own lives but also contributes to the growth and development of their communities.

The impact of Changing Lives with the $150m Secret goes beyond the individuals directly benefiting from the fund. By empowering individuals and communities, the initiative creates a ripple effect that extends to future generations. It breaks the cycle of poverty and creates a pathway for sustainable development and progress.

The Legacy of the $150 Million Secret is a captivating and intriguing story that delves into the world of hidden wealth and the consequences it can have on individuals and society as a whole. This tale unravels the mystery behind a massive sum of money, amounting to a staggering $150 million, that has been kept hidden from the public eye for years.

The story begins with the discovery of a long-lost diary belonging to a wealthy and influential businessman who recently passed away. This diary contains cryptic clues and hints about the existence of a secret fortune, leading a group of determined individuals on a thrilling treasure hunt. As they follow the trail left behind by the deceased businessman, they encounter numerous obstacles and challenges that test their wit, courage, and loyalty.

Throughout the narrative, the author skillfully weaves together multiple storylines, each focusing on different characters who are connected by their pursuit of the hidden wealth. We are introduced to a brilliant and enigmatic detective who is determined to uncover the truth behind the secret fortune, a cunning and manipulative heir who will stop at nothing to claim the money for himself, and a compassionate journalist who becomes entangled in the web of deceit and intrigue surrounding the legacy.

As the characters delve deeper into the mystery, they soon realize that the secret fortune is not just a matter of personal gain, but also holds the potential to impact society in profound ways. The money, if used wisely, could fund charitable organizations, support scientific research, or even alleviate poverty on a large scale. However, in the wrong hands, it could also be used for nefarious purposes, perpetuating corruption and inequality.

The Legacy of the $150 Million Secret explores themes of greed, power, and the ethical dilemmas that arise when faced with the opportunity to possess immense wealth. It raises thought-provoking questions about the responsibility that comes with such fortune and the moral choices individuals must make when confronted with the allure of unimaginable riches.

As the story reaches its climax, the characters are forced to confront their own desires and motivations, ultimately leading to a dramatic and unexpected conclusion. The Legacy of the $150 Million Secret serves as a cautionary tale, reminding us of the potential consequences that can arise from the pursuit of wealth and the importance of integrity and compassion in the face of temptation.

In conclusion, The Legacy of the $150 Million Secret is a captivating and thought-provoking tale that explores the complexities of hidden wealth and its impact on individuals and society.

W. AT'S THE BEST WAY TO READ THIS BOOK?

This book is full of actionable advice based on my own experience. However, you are not forced to read every single chapter to understand the next one. Sometimes, you might not connect with a specific part of the story because you're either too early or too advanced in your journey. If that's the case, simply skip a chapter and get to the next value bomb.

On top of it, I know that time is the most valuable asset you can have as an entrepreneur (or future entrepreneur). That's why I've decided to add a "key takeaways" section at the end of each chapter.

This will allow you to go back to each chapter when you have questions and see what all the important parts are to remember, or if you decide to skip a chapter to have a quick overview of what that chapter talked about.

The chapters of this book also have really straightforward names, so make sure to refer to them if you want to navigate through the book. To start off on the right foot, let's try to deconstruct the biggest lies I've been told my entire life.

5 lies you've bought into from rich/successful people

When I was a kid, I remember that I was fascinated by entrepreneurs on TV. There was something unique about successful people running their businesses.

The sense of relationships, money flowing, the fame, the parties... It felt like they had a secret sauce. Something you can't copy. Something magical.

Coming from the middle class with no entrepreneurs in my family, it felt like launching a business was out of reach.

When I launched (and dramatically failed) my first business with my dad, I really felt like I was missing something... That famous secret sauce that I just mentioned.

I read a lot about it, hoping to find out what I was missing. And after 4 years, I spotted 5 lies that are often told about rich and successful people.

Lie #1: Great ideas make successful businesses

This one is probably the widest spread lie ever, forbidding tons of people worldwide to launch their business.

Usually, people fall into one of the two categories. The ones thinking that they can't start a business because they don't have an idea yet. Or the ones thinking their idea is amazing and don't want to talk about it publicly unless you sign an NDA[2].

Prior to building successful businesses, I was in both categories.

Rich people love this lie because it makes them feel good about themselves. If you only need great ideas to be successful and you're a successful person, it means that you have great ideas. It puts you on a pedestal.

There's nothing wrong with being rich, successful, and getting some acknowledgment for all the work you've done - but this lie prevents a lot of people from even getting started, and it's really frustrating for me.

In the first chapter of the book, we will see why "great ideas" are overrated and also why you don't need a great idea to get your business started!

Lie #2: Risk everything or nothing

I see more and more entrepreneurs telling you that they risked everything they had in order to succeed and that is the only path to success. It's definitely great for storytelling, but what I discovered over time is that it's mostly NOT true...

My feeling about starting a business was the same as getting in a plane to skydive without a parachute.

Skydiving with no parachute

Stating that you're a risk-taker is definitely a great ego boost and the easiest way to feel like a superhero. I remember a so-called business guru telling me:

"If you're not broke or in debt when you launch a business, you won't be able to succeed since you'll feel too comfortable pushing yourself to the limit. It's only when your life depends on your success that you will find the strength to come up with life-changing solutions." Sound familiar?

Well, there are a lot of people out there who will tell you these stories. The truth is that most successful people didn't start out by living the starving entrepreneur life, and there are tons of reasons behind it.

The most important one is that to launch a successful business, you need to sustain yourself and free your brain as much as possible from additional problems you could face in your day-to-day life.

The most successful entrepreneurs I know didn't build their businesses overnight. It took them years of hard work and grind to be able to find something that works. And for that, you need to be able to sustain yourself.

If you are scared to launch a business because you think that to do so, you have to risk everything, well, I feel you.

I was on the same boat years ago. I thought that the only way to succeed was to risk everything.

It frightened me so much that I was waiting for THE best idea… In the end, I was paralyzed and didn't do anything for years.

Skydiving with no parachute

If you've read this far, that's great, you saved the years I spent being paralyzed, too scared to actually launch anything. Because as you probably guessed it, you don't need to risk everything to build a successful business. Will it be easy? No. But the hardest part is to get started.

Human beings are momentum animals. We were only able to evolve as a species because of that momentum. And the best way to give yourself momentum is by taking the first step. The worst thing that can happen is to think about all the ways it can go wrong because you'll fizzle out and won't get started.

In the first chapter of the book, I will show you how to start a business with 0 risks and show you how to be more confident in getting started. So stay tuned!

Lie #3: You need to be ambitious and have a 5-year business

plan to succeed

Marcus Aurelius once said, "A man's worth is no greater than the worth of his ambitions". Well… when I started lemlist in 2018, I wasn't worth a lot.

After I failed my first business with my dad, all I wanted was to be able to launch a business that would get me a decent salary. That was my ambition. Not to build a billion dollar business. I remember feeling bad about it. I thought I should want more.

The truth is that ambition doesn't come naturally. It comes with your surroundings and your confidence to succeed.

Coming from a middle-class family, I had never met incredibly successful people. To me, it was a bit out of reach. And when you think something is out of reach, you clearly don't try to reach it unless you want to die.

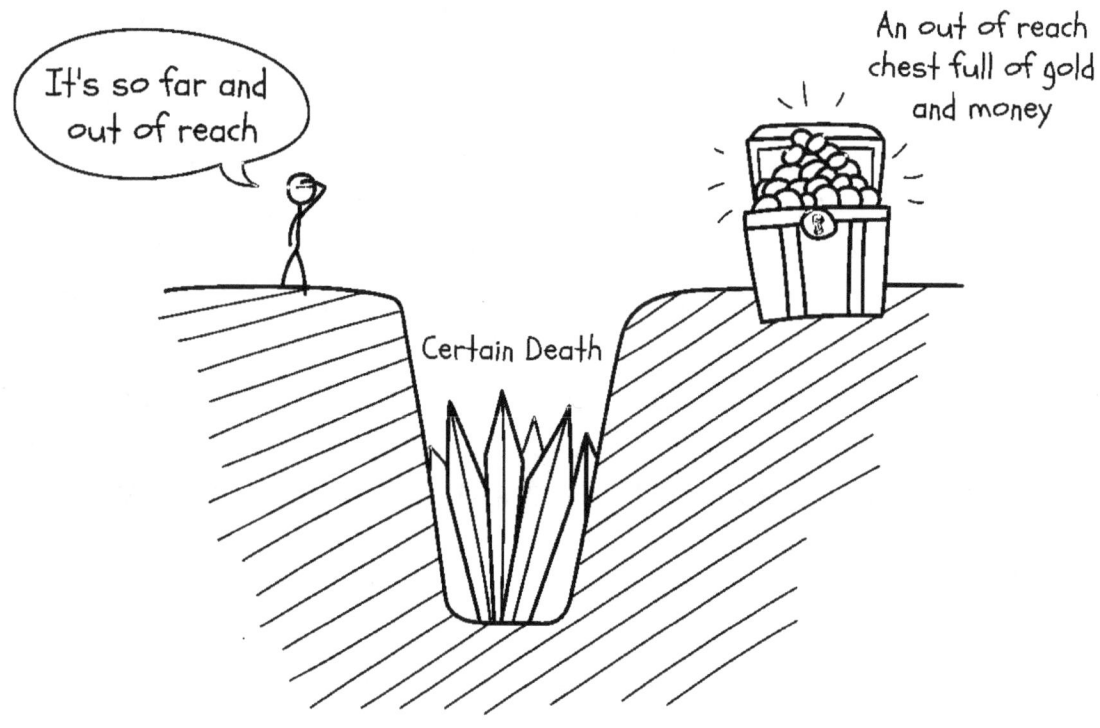

> The truth is that ambition is like appetite. It comes with eating. The more ambitious you are, the more ambitious you will become.
>
> – Guillaume Moubeche

Not being ambitious if you don't have successful people in your family is absolutely fine. Set up smaller goals at first, your ambitions will grow over time.

> The best founders are not the ones who had a 10-year plan, but the ones who could adapt quickly to how the world is changing.
>
> – Guillaume Moubeche

Lie #4: You need a lot of money initially to build a successful business

Most people think that it costs tons of money to start a business. I'm still amazed by the number of blog posts that mention that to start your business, one of the first steps is to get some "love money". Some people even normalize the fact that they got $500,000 from "love money" to start their business.

So-called "love money" is essentially your friends and family giving you money to get started in your business. Clearly, I didn't have the same family or friends as these people.

This image of the rich kid getting $500,000 to start a business is way off and it pisses me off because I know how often people get discouraged by this…

Truth be told, you can actually start becoming an entrepreneur by getting paid, and that's something I will detail in the second chapter. First, let me tell you about the early days of our company, lemlist, a platform that helps startups and small businesses get in touch with their future customers.

We started with $1000. My two co-founders and I each put $333. In the beginning, we struggled a lot. We didn't have money for our salaries, and my girlfriend was paying the rent. My friends and family were always asking me the same question: when are you getting paid?

I felt so much pressure that I stopped visiting my family so I could avoid the embarrassment of saying that I was still broke…

A couple of months after starting lemlist, I met a friend that I hadn't seen for a long time. We sat down to have a coffee and catch up. He asked me, "what's up?" and I told him that I had launched my own start-up. He said, "Oh, nice. How much money did you get from investors?". I told him that we didn't get any. And then he said: "then you don't have a start-up". That's how it works. Apparently, the success of startups depends on how much funds they raise, how much money they receive from investors.

According to the media, the recipe for success is clear: you start a company, raise millions of dollars, get clients, and retire at 35. I had taken the first step, I didn't have millions yet, so I figured why not give it a shot.

I spent 1-month meeting with investors. But it wasn't working. I kept receiving rejection messages: "You haven't done anything yet.", "We don't know you nor your co-founders…", "It's a saturated market, you'll never make it."

But one day, I received the following email from one of our users.

I can't tell you what that meant to me. I had never felt so fulfilled and motivated in my life. At that moment, I knew that I just wanted to recreate that feeling.

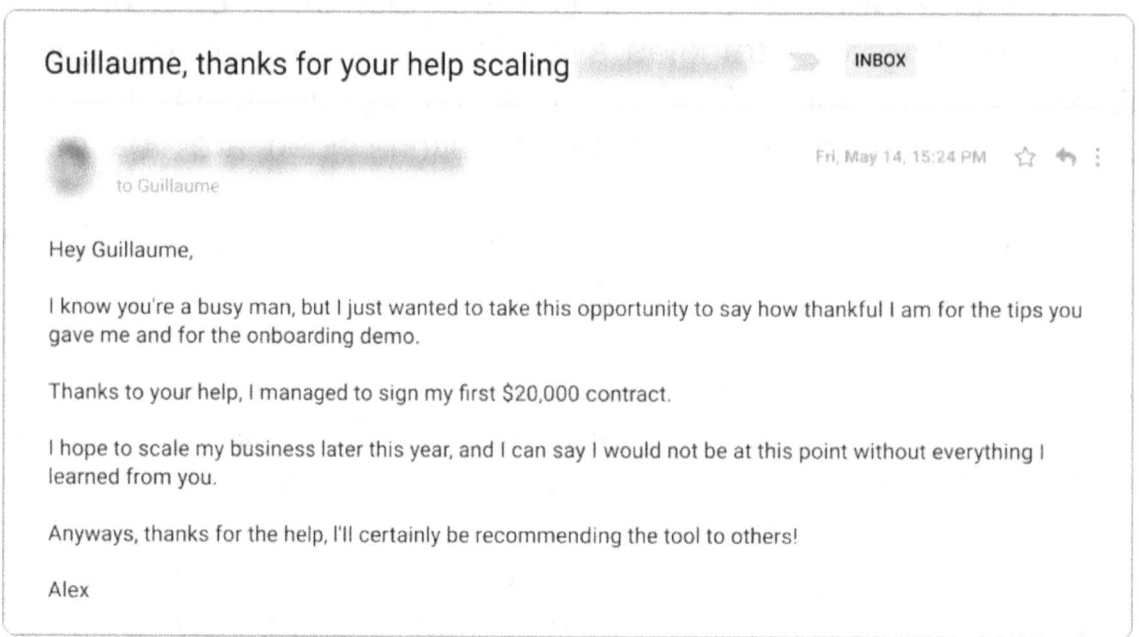

I knew that the moments I felt truly fulfilled and happy was when I was helping other people. That's why I have made it my professional goal and my goal in life to help other people succeed.

So we decided to start lemlist entirely focused on helping others grow their businesses. At the end of our first year, we had thousands of customers all over the world and were starting to earn a decent income. At the end of our second year, I was invited to speak at international conferences about our journey at lemlist.

But before jumping into the details of how we made this happen, here comes the last lie.

Lie #5: In order to build an international company you must raise money

"We're raising $30M so we can expand to the US". You've probably heard this already. The issue with this sentence is that it limits people's ambition. If you think that something is not achievable why would you even try?

Everyone believes that if you want to sell in a specific country or region, you need to have offices there, open a company, etc. Truth is the total opposite.

I feel like with the global COVID crisis, people realized that working remotely was actually working fine and that it was doable to sell pretty much anything over a zoom call.

In the early days of lemlist, I was involved in many US-based communities and we started having people using our product a lot during the beta[3]. When we decided to start a paid plan, we saw that people who were based outside of France would convert at a much higher rate to our paid plan.

After I realized that, I fully focused on the international market and I will detail how we managed to expand in more than 85 countries in 3.5 years. But first, let's discuss the most difficult part of all - how to get started.

G. TTING STARTED

"Start before you're ready." - Steven Pressfield

This quote is probably the best advice anyone could give you and I'm gonna prove it to you, but first let me tell you about one of the greatest basketball players in the world, LeBron James.

In 2003, LeBron James was selected by his hometown team, the Cleveland Cavaliers, as the first overall pick of the NBA draft. At the time, no player of his age had been selected at such a young age and everyone was telling him to continue his education and go to college.

Most people, including his teammates at that time, didn't trust that the 18-years-old high school kid would make an impact or was skilled enough to play in the NBA. More than that, Phil Jackson, who actually was one of the most well-known and respected basketball coaches at the time, said that an 18-year old like James did not belong in the NBA. Most experts at the time had no trust in LeBron's skills and thought that there was too much hype around him.

Despite all the critics and the media pressure, LeBron James punched down all the doubts during his first game scoring 25 points against the Sacramento Kings, setting an NBA record for most points scored by a prep-to-pro player in his debut performance. He beat everyone's expectations, all because he started before he was ready. That same year Lebron James actually got awarded rookie of the year and is now considered by many to be the GOAT[4].

You might be thinking that it was just luck, so let's do the test professor Madson was giving to her students at Stanford.

Close your eyes and imagine a box

Now open the box lid and tell me what's inside.

The magic here is that there's always something inside the box. You can do it another time and the thing inside the box might change BUT there's always something inside. Our unconscious will always provide.

In the end, it doesn't matter if everyone is telling us that we're not ready because our unconscious will always provide a solution. We will always learn new things along the way and grow as a person.

Before we can dive deep into the best way to get started and what mistakes to avoid, I want to go back to years of paralysis. Years of not being able to launch any project on my own…

Why the fear of starting?

Before I started my first business, I was really scared. Scared that I would not be able to generate enough sales to get a salary. Scared that I could lose money. Scared that if I failed, people would look down on me…

I spent months procrastinating, over-preparing, and self-doubting myself for a launch that, in the end, generated 6 sales. I realized that "getting ready" is really comfortable! During this phase, you have no real leap. On top of it, it's quite fun as well because there's no commitment in place.

The issue is that over time, you feel distracted since you don't know what you are doing and therefore you need more time to get ready. This never-ending circle caused many of my friends to freeze and never really get started with anything or launch too late…

> Remember, the enemy is not the work. It's not the difficulty of the work. The enemy is how much your brain will try to resist taking these actions.
>
> – Guillaume Moubeche

Now that you understand "WHY" every entrepreneur felt the fear of getting started at least once in their life, here are a couple of things to help you get started.

1. Trust the process

Getting back to the story of LeBron James, it wouldn't have been possible for him to score a record in his first game if he hadn't taken the leap of going against what people told him to do.

The same applies in business. The more you test new things the more you'll learn and get better at what you do.

2. Momentum is key

When we decide to get started, we turn all our emotions (whether it's fear, passion, ambition, etc.) into energy. This energy is turned into action. And when you take action this is when momentum steps in. To explain momentum in a simple way, you just have to think about going downhill on your bike, you're still going forward without any effort.

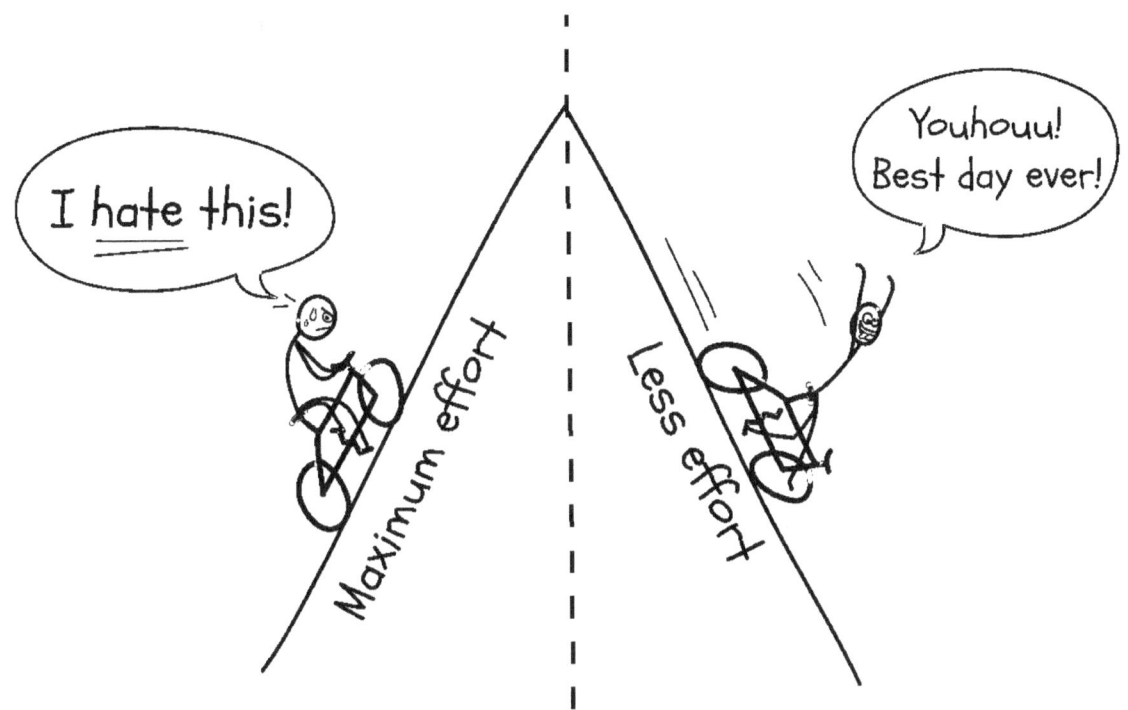

Before you start getting momentum for your business you might wonder whether you should start alone or with someone else. Let's dive into this question.

Alone or with a co-founder?

"If you want to go fast, go alone. If you want to go far, go together" - African proverb

In the last 6 years, I founded or co-founded 5 businesses. One with my dad that failed miserably. One with a friend from business school and an inexperienced developer, where I ended up selling my shares[5]. One on my own where I hired Russian developers, that also failed. Two (lemlist and lempod) with my two technical co-founders[6].

Out of the two, we sold lempod after growing it to $600,000 annual recurring revenue, and we're currently growing lemlist past $10,000,000 in ARR. All of that in only 3.5 years.

During these different experiences, I made a lot of mistakes and I found a few things that worked well. Obviously, what I'm describing in this book is a reflection of my own experience and should be taken as such.

If your goal is to build a SaaS[7] business and you're thinking about getting a co-founder then read on! Finding the right technical co-founder can really be a pain in the a**. The demand for software engineers is extremely high while the supply is really low…

Good software engineers are so rare that they are considered gods. Decent programmers are the prominent majority and they probably receive as many jobs offer as good programmers. There are many more bad programmers than good ones but due to high demand, they tend to also find jobs quite easily. So, how do you meet with your technical co-founder? There is no silver bullet, but let's check out some of the mistakes I made and how you can avoid them.

Mistake #1: You don't know what you don't know…

I joined a startup as a co-founder where the CTO was a bad programmer…at first, my other co-founder (who hired the CTO before I joined) thought our CTO was a Rockstar…

However, after a few months, I realized that every single time we were reporting bugs or trying to define a product roadmap, he was giving us the exact same answer "You know, it's all technical stuff… It's difficult to say how long it will take… It takes time…". If you have no clue about programming it's very difficult to judge how much time a task will take.

Eventually, after talking with other founders and technical experts, we realized that we hired the wrong person for the job...so how do you know if someone is a good developer or not? There are two things you can do.

The first thing is to find someone in your network that has done it already. Ideally, someone technical will be able to help you during the hiring process. If you don't have that person in your network, reach out to existing CTOs of products you like, share your struggle with them and ask them what type of things you should look out for.

Otherwise, if you can't do that, you should ask to check out the projects the programmer has worked on before. Ask him if you can have a look at his GitHub to see the way he has been programming. Is the code commented? Were the projects very similar to one another or different?

After realizing that the CTO was not good enough, we had to let him go and we decided to become a growth agency. Knowing that my goal was to work on a SaaS project I decided to sell my shares in order to start a new project. This time, on my own.

I didn't know any CTO available and I didn't want to spend months looking for one so I decided to hire someone on Upwork. If you don't know UpWork, it's a platform to hire freelancers online. Unfortunately, this is where I made my second mistake.

Mistakes #2: Underpay and no deadlines

Looking at this situation, I want to kick myself in the butt for being so stupid. So I hope that it will help some of you.

At the time, I had very limited resources since I sold my shares of the previous project for about $1,500. My plan was simple: find a freelancer who could build an MVP[8] with the money I got from selling my shares. After that, I would pay him a decent salary and give him shares as soon as we could get the first paying customers.

After doing some research and interviews, I found someone in Russia that was highly motivated.

This guy was actually managing a team of programmers on other projects which meant that he had another source of income.

One month later, the freelancer told me that he liked the project so much that he decided to make all of his teamwork on it. I was super pumped! However, according to the initial roadmap, they were supposed to develop a beta version of the product[9] within 4 to 6 weeks.

After 6 weeks, I could see that some code had been written but there was no beta version of the product as agreed. Once again, there were "good reasons" to explain the delay…

My first mistake here was to pay him on a weekly basis instead of paying him based on specific tasks. But instead of giving up, I decided to meet the team and booked a ticket for 3 weeks in the middle of nowhere Russia.

I was super excited at first…And then I started thinking that I was a bit crazy to do this...but I wanted to be all in!

I really wanted to build a trustworthy relationship with the team and the best way to do it was to meet them in person.

This time, I started implementing another task management system. We broke down each big task into smaller tasks and assigned them to different people on the team. We also added a difficulty level for each task to have more or less an idea of how long each task would take.

Based on those changes, we had 3 weeks to get to a point where I could start testing the product. The objective was very clear... I didn't have enough money to keep paying for something that I couldn't try out and all the team was aware of it.

During the entire development of the project, I also made some very simple documents about the marketing strategy so that everyone could understand the market and why we were developing this project.

I strongly believed that it was important to share the purpose of the project to make people more involved in their work.

I was talking to potential customers every day about the product we wanted to build and I was giving them a link to signup (even though the product didn't exist back then). I would update the number of people who actually left their emails on a whiteboard to be notified when the product would be live to keep the team motivated. Within 3 weeks, we went from 10 to 100 sign-ups on our landing page.

On the relationship side, I got along really well with each team member, even though some of them were not fully fluent in English. It was a really great experience to discover Russian culture! Except for that one night when we came home and realized that the stairs were covered with our neighbor's blood after getting mugged…but that's another story. So now you're probably wondering how it ended up with the team?

Well, since I put this experience in the failed category, you can probably guess that it didn't end up "well", unfortunately. After 3 weeks, we still didn't have a product and I realized that the project was much more technically complex than I thought…

I also realized that you can't expect people to work their asses off if you don't pay them a decent salary. You really pay for what you get when it comes to freelancers. There is no secret in that. My mistake here was not only that I underestimated the cost of such a project, but also that I realized (a bit too late) that I was looking for a REAL partner and not an employee.

During my stay in Russia, I started exchanging ideas with a programmer I met in Station F (a huge startup incubator[10] in Paris) about partnering on a new project. He and his brother were working on a project for 2 years that didn't generate enough revenue to get a salary. They were open to new challenges and I knew that they were really good at coding based on what they had previously built.

What I didn't know at the time was that together we would build a business worth $150,000,000 3.5 years later and sell one of our side-projects during the process. But before getting to that story, let's come back to the main topic. How exactly did I find my two technical co-founders?

Success #1: Trust The Opportunity

When I joined Station F in July 2017, I saw a huge opportunity. I was in THE biggest startup incubator worldwide! I thought that there would be a lot of events to connect, exchange, meet-up, etc. However, in the early days, there were none… So in order to connect with other founders, I offered my help for free whenever I could about topics such as Marketing, User Acquisition, or Growth Hacking.

One day, one of my co-founders asked on the Station F Slack (a messaging tool for the entire Station F community) if someone was willing to help him on a side project to help the Station F community grow and exchange! I was really happy to see that I was not the only one concerned about it, so I decided to help him out. We started brainstorming for a few hours about a side project we could develop so that people could exchange and help one another grow!

After that, I also spent an entire afternoon helping him and his brother out on how they could acquire more users for their SaaS. I outlined different strategies showing them step by step how they could apply them to grow their business. We kept exchanging on various topics and we realized that we shared the same mindset when it came to launching a company. At that time, they were focused on their project and had no intentions to drop it. So we decided to stay in touch.

Fast forward a couple of months, I was working with the Russian team and I asked for their advice several times. This is when we realized the timing was right for all of us.

They knew that I could handle the business side of things and they saw how motivated I was for projects - enough to go to the middle of nowhere in Russia. On my end, I knew they were great programmers who could build anything online.

Our agreement was clear. My two co-founders would develop a beta in 2 weeks and I would find the first 50 beta testers and build a website. After 2 weeks of work, we clearly realized that we were all on the same page and were aligned on the mindset, which convinced us to continue working together.

> The truth is, you never know how and where you're going to meet your co-founders. But the more time you spend meeting people and genuinely helping them, the more likely you will find the right co-founder.
>
> – Guillaume Moubeche

In the end, when launching a startup and finding your co-founders, you need to find the right combination between skills and mindset. It's only when you find people with complementary skills but that have a similar mindset that you know you've found the right partners.

Helping out people whenever you can and working on small projects on the side is literally the only (and best way) to know whether or not you've found the right partners. On top of it, all these "side projects" do not put any pressure and are always fun when you know they are valuable for others!

You might be thinking that finding my co-founders the way I did was a mix of luck and serendipity. You're probably right. But there is more to it. People underestimate what I call business karma.

Success #2: Business Karma

If we go over what happened with my two co-founders, here is what we get:

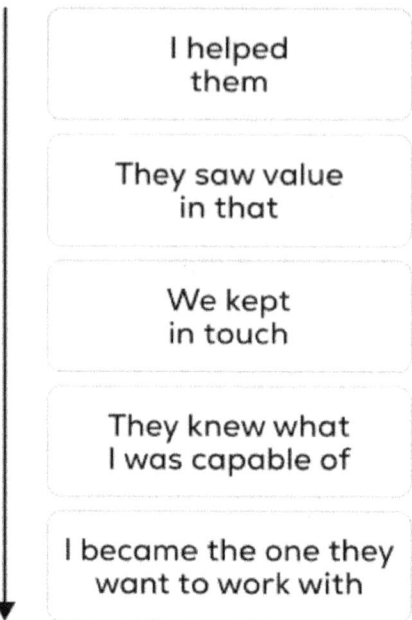

Something I took a lot of time to realize is that doing things you're passionate about will never feel like work. I see a lot of people trying to guilt others when they have "work" ideas at night, during parties, or playing sports…

> But the truth is that when you're passionate about what you do, you'll never feel like you're working.
>
> – Guillaume Moubeche

And if what you do involves helping people, then you'll never have a day without motivation or drive. The more you focus on helping people, the more positive things will happen to you. It works exactly the same way in life and in business.

However, looking back at this story with my two co-founders, I realized that we might have never met if we were not both at Station F. That's why I want to share a secret with you. Something that will make people want you to be their co-founders.

Documenting everything to find the co-founder

There's a secret way of making sure that you can attract the best developers for your project. That secret is called "Marco Polo".

Not sure if you remember that game we used to play when we were kids. One person is chosen to be "it" and they close their eyes and get in one end of the swimming pool. They count to 10 and shout "Marco," and all the others in the pool shout "Polo." The one that shouts "Marco" has to try and catch one of the people who shouts "Polo". Well, that's not what I want to talk about. I want to talk about Marco Polo, the famous explorer.

Marco Polo spent years traveling and discovering the unknown silk roads. Years of meeting with new people and discovering new cultures. Years of documenting all of the things no one knew about in Europe. Years of documenting the unknown in his book called "The travels of Marco Polo".

The only issue here is that Marco Polo was NOT an explorer at all…he was like most Venetians at that time, a merchant. He wasn't the first one to discover new cultures in the East nor the first one to discover the famous "silk road". However, everyone thought he was.

So why is he remembered as the one who discovered it first? Simple. He was the first to document his journey.

This leads us to the next part where we'll see why teaching can help you become the "Marco Polo" of your industry (don't worry, we're not going back to school!).

Becoming a teacher

Now you're probably saying, that's cool G. but Marco Polo had some amazing stories to tell since he was traveling all the time. True. But look at any industry and find the most known people. What do they all have in common? They teach. Not in the way a teacher would do in front of a whiteboard. They do it through blogging, videos, posts on social media, newsletters, etc.

Teaching is the best way to position yourself as a thought leader. Why? Because you bring value to people. You help them understand a topic they didn't know about. This is usually when people tell me one of the two things:

1. I'm not an expert in anything so how could I write about it?

2. Nothing interesting ever happened to me

So here's what I usually answer:

1. If you had to write a blog post about how to launch a

rocket on the moon? What would you do?

I'm guessing that you'd search on Google about how a rocket works, how to launch it, from where, how much it will cost, etc., and then write about it! Well…it's the same thing with your business.

Every great entrepreneur and content creator knows that they don't know everything but that they can learn everything. It's pretty simple, to be seen as a thought leader you simply need to teach.

Teach people what you've learned and you'll quickly become an expert. On top of that, teaching is also the best way to learn and master a new topic as it forces you to transform all the information you've read, watched, or listened to and turn it into your own ideas.

Teaching and documenting everything will force you to have more clarity. As David Perrell once said, "Read to collect the dots and write to connect them".

2. Once we learn something it becomes obvious. That's why we feel like it is not worth talking about it.

You just have to look at how amazed kids are when they see someone on a bike. "How the hell can they go faster than me walking on something that doesn't hold itself?!" But for you, riding a bike doesn't need an explanation right?

Well, it's the same way with your entrepreneurial journey or pretty much any journey where you'll learn something.

Everything you've learned and experienced could have helped the younger and less experienced version of yourself. Even though it looks obvious to you now.

As an entrepreneur, here are a few things that are easy to document:

- Why did we want to work on this project?
- How did we get our first beta testers?
- How did we get our first customers?
- Why did we decide to work on that specific project?
- What do we want to accomplish in the next X years?
- What struggles did we face working in the X industry?
- What are our learnings after X months of being entrepreneurs?

And the list goes on and on…

Celebrate milestones, wins, struggles and talk about them freely.

You're probably wondering how this ties to finding the right technical co-founder right? Well, remember how my two co-founders, and I built our relationship? We got to meet each other, and it's only because I was updating them on what I was doing that they realized what I could do.

Writing and documenting everything you do is doing the exact same thing, but with a much larger audience, hence at scale.

> By documenting everything you learn and do, and sharing your unique story with others, you become the person people want to meet.
>
> – Guillaume Moubeche

Let's take this book as an example. By now, you must feel like you know me better. And you're right. You know how many businesses I've launched, the ones that I failed, etc. We created this relationship through my writing. And you can do exactly the same thing.

Positioning yourself as a thought leader and documenting your journey will help you to connect with people at scale and opportunities will keep flowing your way, but we will discuss this in more detail a little bit later in the second and third chapters. First, let's recap the key learnings of this chapter.

Key learnings

- The enemy is not the work, nor the difficulty of the work. The enemy is how much your brain will try to resist in taking action.
- You don't know what you don't know.
- The more you'll test new things the more you'll learn and get better at what you do.
- Momentum is key.
- The more time you spend meeting up with people and genuinely helping them, the more likely you will find the right co-founder.
- When launching a startup and finding your co-founders, you need to find the right combination between complementary skills and mindset.
- When you're passionate about what you do, you'll never feel like you're working.
- The more you focus on helping people, the more positive things will happen to you.
- Teaching is the best way to position yourself as a thought leader. It's also the best way to learn and master a new topic, as it forces you to transform all the information you've read, watched or listened to and turn it into your own ideas.
- Positioning yourself as a thought leader and documenting your journey will help you to connect with people at scale and bring new opportunities your way.

I. EA

I was chatting with a friend of mine the other day. To give you more context, she's been working as the Head of Growth of a well-known startup for years and her dream is to launch her own company.

However, she always tells me the exact same thing: "I'm looking for the right idea to get started". And I always answer "you're making excuses to postpone starting". Not judging…I've been there as well!

I spent months trying to figure out what the best idea was before launching a t-shirt brand with my dad. Months trying to figure out what would work best and finding excuses to postpone the launch. I was convinced that we couldn't launch because our website was not perfect. Because our community was not big enough. Because we didn't have enough t-shirt stock, etc. The last one was probably the biggest lie I told myself when you see that we only sold 6 t-shirts when we finally launched…

In the end, this t-shirt business failed not because of the idea but because of the poor execution. Execution is the number one factor of success. When you see that people can make a million-dollar business selling rocks with a face drawn on them - you understand the power of good execution. So if you don't need a good idea to get started, what should you focus on first?

Stop looking for ideas - start looking for problems to solve

Do you know that billion-dollar company called "The idea marketplace", where people are selling their ideas? No? Really? Well, that's because it doesn't exist. Ideas don't sell.

However, solving problems does. And that's how most successful businesses are built. But let's face it, it's always a struggle to find the right problem to solve. Do you know why?

Let's imagine that you don't brush your teeth for three days. If you start talking in a crowded room, everyone will probably smell your bad breath. But you won't. Even though your mouth is just right under your nose…

That's the same thing with problems. We tend not to notice nor remember the problems we are facing on a daily basis.

Let me tell you a story about an Italian tractor manufacturer, born to vigneron in Renazzo. His company was successful enough so he could afford to drive a Ferrari, but he got frustrated by the size of the clutch. He decided to visit the one and only Enzo Ferrari. He tried to explain his pain and expected Enzo Ferrari to take it into consideration to improve his Ferrari cars. But here was Ferrari's answer: "Let me make cars. You stick to making tractors." Really pissed by his answer, the tractor manufacturer decided to launch his own sports car brand. His name? Ferruccio Lamborghini.

In 2020 Lamborghini was valued at $11 billion - not bad for a tractor manufacturer! What pushed Ferrucio to launch his company was a pain/frustration he was experiencing.

> We tend to focus on others' problems when the best way to launch a business is to focus on our own problems.
>
> – Guillaume Moubeche

If you look at my entrepreneurial journey so far, I tried to focus as much as possible on the problems that I was facing.

I built a lead generation agency to help people find their next customers because I couldn't find customers with the t-shirt brand I built with my dad.

I wanted to build lemlist because all the tools I was using for the agency were not allowing me to personalize my sales prospecting enough to build better relationships.

I wanted to build lempod because I was frustrated with manually interacting with my friend's LinkedIn post URLs and I thought we could automate that.

Focusing on problems I was facing gave me the confidence of knowing that it will be helpful to me and knowing that something that is helpful to you is, in my opinion, the best way to get started. First, because you'll be your first user and best critic. Second, because with the ups and downs of entrepreneurship, when you know that what you're working on is helpful, it gives you enough courage to continue no matter what. And on top of it, let's face it, with 7 billion people on the planet, if it's helpful to you it will also be helpful to thousands of other people too.

But before focusing on the problem you can face, here's the best way to find more problems and build a successful business from the start. It comes down to that secret formula that I called Service Audience Success.

Service audience success

A lot of people, especially in the tech world, hate the idea of creating a service business. They think that it is not scalable because, in the end, you'll end up charging for peoples' time no matter what you do. True.

But building a service business is, in my opinion, the best and easiest way for anyone to get started at entrepreneurship. Service will teach you the most important skill in building a successful business. If you know how to help people solve their problems, you'll always be successful.

When I launched my lead generation business, I had no clue how to do sales prospecting. But I knew that finding customers was a pain for many businesses. I knew it because that's how I failed my first business with my dad.

So I started to reach out to people asking them if they wanted to get more meetings with potential customers. At the time I had very limited knowledge of how to do it. But once I saw that I could convince people that I was the right person to do it for them and that I was getting paid to do it, I instantly knew that this service was bringing value to people.

I spent a lot of time online learning how to do sales prospecting while I had clients paying me to do it. Pretty sweet right? As our business started scaling I was able to touch base on customer support, sales, marketing, and hence, pretty much all the aspects of running a business.

The reason why selling services is so cool is because it allows you to get paid to learn a new skill. Once you've convinced someone that you can achieve something, you have a much stronger motivation to learn how to become the best at it and deliver results.

Earlier in this book, I explained why most people are afraid to get started with entrepreneurship because they feel like they need to risk it all. That fear of the famous "leap of faith". Risk it all or die…

In reality, anyone could run a business. But most people are afraid they won't be able to make money out of it. Which makes sense.

We grew up our entire life with the traditional path of going to school, studying as long as possible to get the best degree, and then getting a good, safe job.

Starting something on your own is "new" by definition, and therefore scary for most people...

But starting as a freelancer or building an agency is literally the best thing anyone who's scared to get started can do. It allows you to break that false belief that you won't be able to generate money on your own. Once you know that, anything can become possible.

If you're wondering what you can do to get started with that route, here are some skills you can learn online that don't require any particular prior skills:

- Copywriting
- Ads → you can even niche it to Facebook Ads, Google Ads, Pinterest Ads, LinkedIn Ads, etc.
- Cold emailing[11]
- Web Design (building websites)
- SEO (Search Engine Optimization)[12]
- Email Marketing[13]
- Social Media Marketing

And the list goes on.

If you feel like this is a path you want to try out, you have two options. The first one is to learn a skill and then get started. The second one is to start and then learn the skill. If you remember the first chapter, you know what I'm gonna say. Get started first!

Let's take the example where you've decided to learn how to do Facebook ads.

To get started, I would go into a Facebook group of entrepreneurs or startups and write something like:

By doing this, you'll create a viral post, since you're offering something really valuable for free.

Once everyone starts commenting, the post will get more and more reach allowing you to get even more people interested. You can also ask a couple of friends to comment at first in order to boost the initial reach.

To make it simple, the virality of a Facebook post depends on its engagement. The more engagement, the more people will actually see the post.

Comments have a bigger impact on the virality of a Facebook post vs giving a "like" because when people comment on a post, it means that they are spending more time on Facebook.

The more time a user spends on Facebook, the more money Facebook makes.

The business model of any social media platform is to make money through advertising. And to be able to sell advertising you need to have active users. For Facebook, the more active their users are, the more money they can make.

So when someone comments on a post, it means, for the Facebook algorithm, that the content is engaging. Therefore the post will be rewarded by being showcased to an even larger audience. If the larger audience engages, then the post can become viral.

Let's go back to our post where we asked people to comment in order for you to help them for free. Based on all the engagement on the post, you'll then be able to select the project you like the most. In that case, I would ask people how much they want to spend on ads, what the company's revenue is, etc.

The idea here is to be able to spot your future clients, so you need to make sure that the company is already making a decent amount of money and that they have a real budget for ads.

Now that you have your first customers, this is when you spend hours learning a new skill and putting every single thing you learn into practice. At that stage, you should pick 2 to 5 companies at first so you can really deliver results.

Once you start seeing results you ask them to hop on a Zoom call and record it so you can get a testimonial and build a success story.

Here are a few questions to ask during the recorded call:

1. Can you describe the problem you were facing before you actually started working with me?
2. Can you please detail the frustrations you were experiencing when trying to solve this problem?
3. Can you please describe the moment you understood that my service was the solution to the problem you were facing?
4. What does your day-to-day look like now that this problem has been solved?

With testimonials and success stories, you're one step away from having a real business in less than a month. The next step? Get paid!

Remember that Facebook group where you posted in, well it's time to go back and start documenting and sharing your story! Here's something you could write:

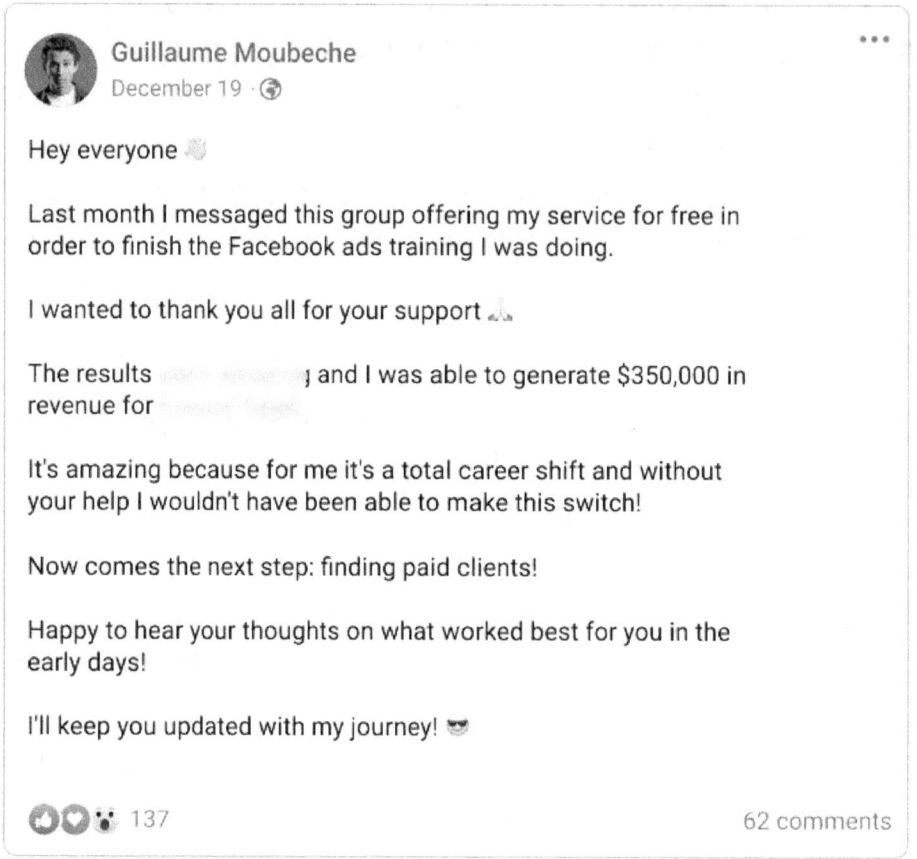

By doing so you're doing 2 things:

1. Making your journey a common effort as you're showing gratitude to the community

2. Attracting potential new customers because you've shown that you did a great job with one of your clients, so some people might reach out to you directly

Testimonials are an amazing way to acquire new clients as it shows that you're someone they can trust to get their desired results. In parallel, you should also get in touch with the people you worked with and let them know that you are now launching your Facebook ad agency. And based on the results you brought them, it'll be easy to start asking for money for your service.

Now that you have your agency and you started making money, you have done the most difficult part of all: getting the confidence that you can make money on your own without having to work for an employer. You're finally financially free!

Eventually, you'll start getting more clients than you can handle, and this is when you decide to outsource some of the work. You'll be able to manage a team of people, know how to acquire clients, and provide good customer support. All of these **three skills are essential for an entrepreneur to grow any business.**

Along this journey of growing a service and building an audience, you're gonna start to feel frustrated with many things, or have conversations with people who are frustrated with things you didn't even notice.

It can either come from the tools you use, the processes or even some administrative stuff.

Once you focus on all the frustrations and problems, you'll start to think about solutions. **These solutions will be your next "big idea"!**

As you grow your business, you should document everything. Build a personal brand[14] as soon as possible so that when you decide to look for a technical co-founder they can look at your profile and think, "OK, this person knows what they're talking about!"

When I launched lemlist, I didn't have an audience. I had to build it from scratch and it took a lot of time. But eventually, after a year and a half of posting consistently on LinkedIn and writing blog articles, I became an industry leader in the sales automation industry.[15]

I was invited to be a speaker at many events internationally and each of my LinkedIn posts reached between 20,000 and 200,000 people.

By building this audience I was able to learn 2 things:

1. your network is your net worth (for real)

2. the more you post things online the more people trust you

The more people trust you, the easier it is for them to buy something from you.

I remember in the early days of lemlist, I was really struggling to get initial traction. People didn't know me so it took about a year to build a big-enough audience to start getting real traction.

However, when we launched our second software a year after, lempod, I started to build an audience: the traction was immediate. What took us a year to achieve with lemlist only took us 3 months with lempod. I was amazed that simply because people knew me and knew that I was always providing value - they all wanted to test this new tool we had built.

My two co-founders coded the first version of lempod in 2 days during a conference and after four days we already had 100+ users. By the end of the first month, we had 1000 users and after 3 months we were making as much money as we did with lemlist after 1 year.

Building an audience prior to lemlist while I had my agency is definitely something that I should have done. So if you're at the stage of building your agency, or working at a startup, always remember to focus on building an audience as soon as possible. In my case, it would have allowed us to get huge traction from day 1 just like what we had for lempod.

Remember the "finding your co-founder" part? Well, now that

you know why and how to build an audience, I can assure you that this will not be an issue.

With a strong audience, finding your technical co-founder will be a piece of cake (this also works the other way around if you're a tech guy looking for a business partner).

The essence of any business relationship, whether we're talking about client relationships or co-founders relationships, is trust. By building an audience by providing value to people and sharing your journey, you become the person people want to meet and work with. Why? Because they feel like they know you and hence, trust you.

Let's say that you grew your audience so much that you now found the perfect problem to solve. You're probably wondering how to validate your business idea? But more importantly...

How to validate an idea quickly?

The only way to really validate an idea is to get your customers to pay for your solution, product, or service. Before that, having people tell you that they'd pay for it is just words. Words and promises don't pay for food or rent.

However, when building a tech product, getting to that point of having people paying for your SaaS can take time, and that's why having other indicators of initial validation is a good way to go.

Crowded market

In the last few years, I've built 2 SaaS products. One was in a super crowded market (lemlist) and the other one was in an empty market (lempod).

It's funny how most people think that because a market is crowded you shouldn't go there…the truth is that a crowded market is literally the best way to validate your idea quickly. Why?

Because a crowded market shows that people are actually paying for the solution to the problem you want to solve. If you want to succeed in a crowded market you need to be better than the competition. And being better is often being different. That's called positioning.

Let's take the email marketing industry for example. MailChimp is clearly leading the game with newsletters. So most people would think that they shouldn't go there as they are tens of thousands of competitors! The truth is that you could build yourself a really strong brand by being super niche in your positioning.

For example, you could start a newsletter tool only for people selling online courses. It's very niche, so your messaging will resonate 10x better with your audience. Let's take a look at how messaging works. Say that you're an entrepreneur and you need to choose a bank between a random bank and a bank for startups, which one would you choose

Well, I guess you'll go for the bank for entrepreneurs because you naturally think that it's a better fit for you. That's the power of niches.

Now you're probably thinking: "great G. but if I focus on a niche I would never be able to build a billion-dollar company because the size of my market would be too small!" Let me answer that doubt with the story of Apple.

In the early days, they focused on creating the best personal computers for designers. Their positioning was super niche. But as they grew, they built a movement around creativity. They associated the Apple brand with "Creativity". So people using Apple products started to feel like they were part of the "creative class". Their niche focus became a differentiator people wanted to be part of. That's why they were able to grow outside of their niche with their "Think Different" tagline and become a trillion-dollar company. You got the point - being different works!

This leads us to the second option: empty market. You might also see the terminology "Blue Ocean" for such markets which essentially means that there is no competitor or business addressing a specific problem.

Empty market

If a market is empty with no competitors it means 3 things:

1. your competitors are too small to be found yet.
2. with 7 billion people on the planet, the chances of multiple people having the same ideas are very very high. So it might be that the people who have tested the same thing as you want to achieve have failed.
3. the timing was not right before and you're onto

something really cool!

So how to validate your idea quickly in an empty market?

You need to find out whether or not people are facing the same problem as you do. That's when social networks are literally a gold mine. Go to Quora, Reddit, or any Facebook group where your target audience is and ASK PEOPLE the question.

For example, let's say that you find it super frustrating for people to go back and forth organizing a meeting via email.

You could ask people in communities if they are facing the same problem and whether or not they think it would be valuable for them to have a link where people could see each other's availability and directly book a spot? By the way, this product already exists, it's called Calendly and it's a multi-billion-dollar company now.

When asking people about whether or not they might be facing a specific problem you get a sense of the usefulness of your idea. But it's not enough to validate a business idea. Remember that it's only when people will actually pay for your product or service that you will have true validation.

However, you can get another type of validation by pretending that you already built the solution and that you're looking for feedback and beta testers.

You can easily create a "viral post" in a community where your niche hangs out and be able to start building your email list at the same time for the launch.

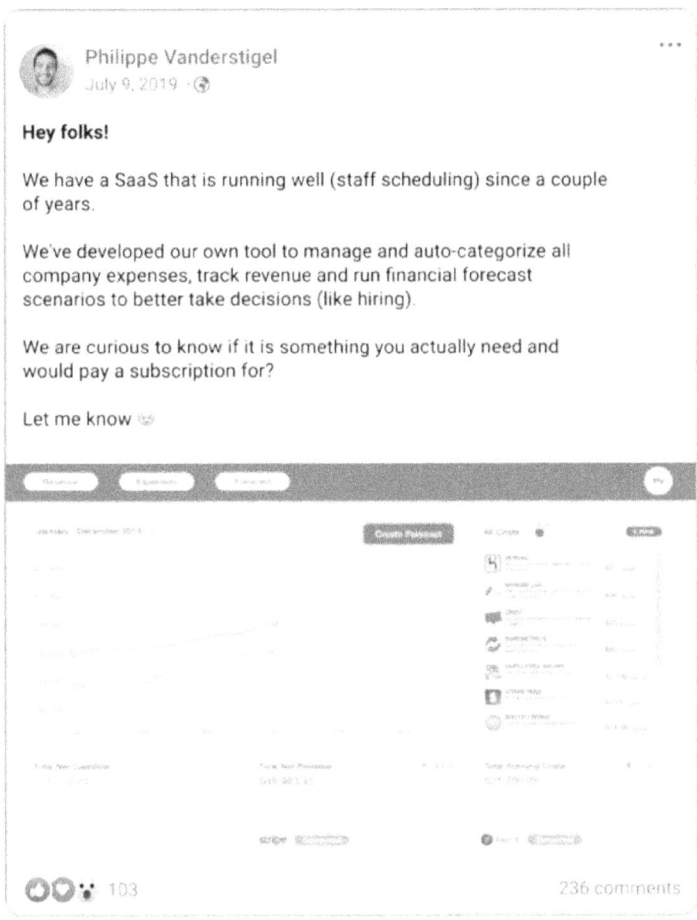

In this example, Philippe is asking people to comment if they'd be interested in joining the beta of a tool he "built". Truth to be told, the tool was not ready yet, but Philippe had designed what he wanted it to look like so he pretended that the tool was ready.

By doing so and adding an image showcasing the tool (which didn't exist at the time), it made people picture themselves using the tool and perceive the value. The more people commented, the more people saw the post and hence the more virality the post got. And with 236 comments, it was a pretty good first step validation and also a great way for Philippe to get hundreds of conversations with potential future clients.

Now that you know how to validate your idea quickly, comes the time to actually grow your business. And when growing a business, a few opportunities arise including whether or not you should take external funding. So, let's talk about bootstrapping.

The art of bootstrapping

In the last few years, the rise of successful bootstrapped companies keeps increasing and we started seeing more and more people being attracted to this way of growing a company.

With all the VC[16] backed startups getting 99% of the press coverage in tech, in this chapter we'll discuss what bootstrapping is and the differences between each model.

What is bootstrapping?

Bootstrapping a business means growing your business with very limited resources, and hence with no outside help nor intake of capital from investors.

For example, we started lemlist with only $1000. My two co-founders and I each put $333 to launch the company.

Bootstrapping means that to grow your business, the only money you will get is from your customers (or banks). And as you probably guessed, growing a bootstrapped company vs a VC-backed one is very different, and we'll dive into the reasons "why".

Funding VS bootstrapped

In the early days of my journey as a SaaS entrepreneur, I was 100% convinced that in order to experience hyper-growth and build a successful company, **you had** to get money from investors.

If you look at what we see on a daily basis in most tech media, the more money people get from investors, the more articles you'll see. However, 75% of companies who have raised funds, which means those who got money from investors…fail. That's 8 out of 10. But how can you get millions and still end up with nothing? To me, it's simple.

A company is like a cake. Un gateau. At the start, each co-founder has a piece of that cake. When an investor wants to give money to a company, it's generally for 2 reasons: First, they want a piece of the gateau. Second, they want to use the money they give to cook a bigger cake. Un gros gateau.

So why is it that those companies fail? I'm going to tell you why. It's because it is way more complicated to cook when there is another Chef in the kitchen! Can you make the cake of your dreams, if someone tells you which ingredients to use?

When you start taking investment, you don't have the same flexibility in the way you handle your business. Obviously, it depends a lot on the investors but what most people don't understand when raising funds, is that money has a cost.

The goal of most investors is to get 10x on each of their investments. So if they invest at a $100,000,000 valuation, they expect the company to be worth at least $1 billion in the next 4 years.

These expectations will add extra pressure on the founders and in my opinion, sometimes it pushes some companies to fail.

Let me tell you a story about an inventor named Samuel

Pierpont Langley. Langley had raised a lot of money from the government and as you can imagine, was getting tons of media attention and exposure.

Everywhere he was going, he was followed by the teams of the most prestigious journals. Why? He was convinced that his new invention would change the face of the world. He wanted to build the first airplane.

Langley attempted to fly on October 7th, 1903. Everyone was convinced that he would succeed so every media channel was there. He had even prepared a catapult to launch his "flying machine". But when he first attempted it, the "flying machine" fell into the water like a sack of cement.

On December 8th, after 2 months of hard work and trying to understand why he didn't work the first time, Langley attempted another time. This time with much more confidence. But despite Langley's effort, he failed another time.

What no one knew at the time is that hundreds of kilometers away from Langley's failed attempt, two brothers, called the Wright brothers, were able to fly an airplane for the first time in history. No journalist was there. No media coverage. No fanfare. Just two passionate brothers that made their dream come true through hard work and focus.

To me, this story illustrates why fundraising is not a recipe for success and why bootstrapping can sometimes win. I'm not against fundraising in any way, and I think that for some companies it's actually mandatory if they want to grow or conquer new markets. But if you've decided to bootstrap your company you should always remember the Wright Brothers' story.

It is possible for a bootstrapped business to be more successful than a VC-backed one, even if at first you think that money was a competitive advantage. You can find hundreds of examples out there, so never get discouraged or lower your ambitions because you are bootstrapping.

> Raising money will give you fame and attention. But fame will not always bring you success.
>
> – Guillaume Moubeche

The bootstrapped journey is a different one and should be treated as such. Therefore there are a few rules to live by.

3 rules to live by as a bootstrapped entrepreneur

When growing a business I feel like you should always have rules to live by. These rules will evolve during the different stages of your business, but to me, they are key to define early on and I'll show you why.

Rule #1 Make money fast

Asking people to pay for your product is the scariest thing to do as a founder. You feel like your product is not good enough. That it doesn't yet deliver the value you'd want it to deliver. That it needs more development work…

> The only true validation of a business comes from when you start generating revenue from it. Period.
>
> — Guillaume Moubeche

I can't tell you how many arguments one of my co-founders and I had about that. I was always pushing the payment deadline because I wanted the product to have more features.

I told him that it was not ready and that people won't see enough value to pay. That we should gather more feedback and do more interviews…the truth is, I was scared. Scared that no one would pay. Scared that all the work we had put in was useless…scared to be a failure again…

On the other hand, having launched many SaaS products in the past, he knew that it was the only way to get real validation. He knew that without having paying customers people could tell you pretty much anything they want in order to make you feel good about what you're building. He knew that it was the only way to really start calling our project a business. And he was 100% right!

With time I've realized how wrong I was! Even if it is scary at first, it's extremely important to ask people to pay for your product or service! And since we're on the "money" topic, let's jump right into "rule #2".

Rule #2 Pay yourself first - increase your salary often

This rule was probably the most difficult rule to live by for me.

Being in charge of the business side of things, I've always wanted to invest the earnings as much as possible back into the business. When you live with very little money, you get used to it and what matters the most in your eyes is the growth of the business.

However, with my two co-founders being older than I, and with different needs in life - we decided to set this rule as something we must follow no matter what: we need to increase our salary often so the growth of the company should be tied to our own revenue growth.

When I look back at this decision, I really think that this was one of the reasons why we grew so fast. As the company's revenue grew, we were increasing our salary every quarter. And what I realized was that the more money we were making on an individual level, the more ambitious we became.

If you're getting a salary that, step by step, becomes way higher than what you could actually spend in a month, then you start valuing things differently. For example, the more you earn each month the more you realize how valuable your time is. With that in mind, every decision you take pushes you to think big. You're basically pushing your norm and can take much more risks.

On top of it, as you're growing your company you'll have more cash at your disposal to take more risks. However, on our end, we always wanted to focus on profit and I'll explain why in the next rule.

Rule #3 Your superpower is profitability

A lot of people ask me what is the #1 metric I look at each month. To me, it's profitability[17].

One of the main differences between a VC-backed business and a bootstrapped business often lies in that point. If investors gave you money, they expect you to spend it to fuel the growth. This usually means hiring more people.

With their logic, the more people you hire, the faster you'll grow. While this might be true in some service-based businesses, I think that hiring too quickly, especially in tech companies, can make your startup fail.

The faster you hire people, the more mistakes you'll make and the more diluted your culture will become. On top of it, the more people in a company the less efficient you'll become (more meetings, more middle management, a longer chain of command, less adaptability - you get the point). This can be really frustrating for a lot of highly talented people who prefer doing real things rather than spending hours in meetings.

For these VC-backed startups, fundraising means spending more money than what you earn in order to accelerate and fuel the growth. This model based on not being profitable can work well in some cases; think of Amazon and Uber for example - however, it puts a lot more stress on the company. Why? Because when you're not profitable and hence losing money every single month - you have a deadline on how long your company can last.

Let me give you an example: If you have $1,000,000 in your bank account and each month you are spending $200,000 more than what you are earning - you'll have a survival rate of 5 months. After that, you have to raise money again if you want to survive.

What most startups try to do is to reach break-even before they have spent the entire money they've raised so they can raise another round of funding under the best terms possible. If you can't reach that break-even point, then you put yourself under more pressure because it means that your company's survival will only rely on whether or not you can raise funding.

To give you some context, a friend of mine had raised 10s of millions to grow his startup. They were losing millions each month in order to fuel the growth. Their only goal was to drive growth and they will never care about profitability. They were convinced that their investors would always follow them and hence add more money at each round of fundraising.

After 4 years and 3 different rounds, they had complete trust in their investors. However, when they needed to plan for the fourth round of fundings, some investors told them 2 weeks before they ran out of cash that they wouldn't put money at the expected valuation. Instead, they divided the startup valuation by two. They had no other option than to say yes but got diluted twice as much (meaning that they had to give 2 times more shares to the investors). On top of that, they had lost the most important thing: the trust in their investors.

A year later, they ran out of cash and decided to stop their business. That business was valued hundreds of millions of dollars, yet, the founders ended up with nothing (and the investors as well).

I'm not saying that all stories with fundraising end up like that. But most do. Like every startup, there's always a huge risk. And being profitable is literally the best way to hedge that risk. Why?

> Because once you become profitable as a SaaS, technically, your business has an infinite lifetime.
>
> – Guillaume Moubeche

It's very rare for a SaaS business to have a down month - meaning a month where you would make less money than the previous one.

The reason is that most SaaS actually bill their customers a monthly subscription fee. So the more customers you acquire the higher your MRR[18] will be. That's literally the beauty of any recurring business model[19]. That's why it gives you that infinite lifetime that you should always aim for.

To me, profitability is essential because I want to make sure that everyone from the team can get paid at the end of the month. By knowing that we're profitable each month I have literally zero mental weight when it comes to money. And as a founder the more you can remove mental weight from your day-to-day, the better!

Now that you have the perfect idea with the perfect co-founders, it's time to get your business off the ground.

Key learnings

- Execution is the number one factor of success.
- The best way to launch a business is to focus on our own problems.
- Service will teach you the most important skill in building a successful business.
- Knowing that something is helpful to you is the best way to get started.
- With testimonials and success stories, you can quickly escalate your business growth.
- As you grow your business, document everything.
- Your network is your net worth.
- The more you post things online the more people trust you. The more people trust you, the easier it is for them to buy something from you.
- The essence of any business relationship, whether we're talking about client relationships or co-founders relationships, is trust. By building an audience by providing value to people and sharing your journey, you become the person people want to meet and work with.
- The only way to really validate an idea is to get your customers to pay for your solution, product, or service.
- A crowded market is literally the best way to validate your idea quickly.
- Bootstrapping means that to grow your business, the only money you will get is from your customers (or banks).
- Raising money will give you fame and attention. But fame will not always bring you success.
- The only true validation of a business comes from

when you start generating revenue from it.
- Hiring too quickly, especially in tech companies, can make your startup fail.
- The faster you hire people, the more mistakes you'll make and the more diluted your culture will become.
- Once you become profitable, your business technically has an infinite lifetime.

B□.L□

In the previous chapters, you've learned the steps prior to launching your SaaS business, you understand why it's so important to build an audience and so that everyone with who you've connected wants to be part of your next adventure. Now, it's time to build!

Building a business is like getting the keys to a motorcycle that is laying down on the ground. To get started, first, you need to pull it up from the ground and that's what requires the heavy lifting.

In this chapter, we'll see the most important phases to build a successful business and how to go from 0 to getting your first customers.

Build something you want

If you've been watching a few of the very well-known videos, interviews, or keynotes from YC founder Sam Altman, you must know that in order to build a successful startup you need to "Make something people want". This mantra might apply to "unicorns" (a business with a valuation of $1B or more), but building one is not everyone's goal.

I'm a firm believer that making something YOU really want is the best way to get started! Especially if you get started with what we call a "side project". A side project is basically a project that will not require your full focus. It's something that you could do on top of your existing job or while running your company.

If you take the example of lempod, the second SaaS project we built, that's exactly what it was. A project we knew we really wanted to build but that at the same time, will not take all of our time so we could still be focused on our main project: lemlist.

At the time, I was in a few communities where people would share the link to their LinkedIn posts in order to get more engagement from the community. Since communities are by essence a place where you want to help people, I would click on each link to like and comment on their posts in order to support creators and founders. In exchange, people would also do the same when I would post something. But clicking on every link was really time-consuming and I thought that we could automate that process.

I started discussing with my two co-founders in order to evaluate the complexity of creating a chrome extension to do that automatically. 48 hours later, they built an MVP.[20]

I decided to go back to these same communities where everyone posted the link to their posts and I told them about the new tool we had built. 5 days after that we had 100 users on lempod.

As you can see, I did the opposite of what every single business book out there would tell you to do. I didn't do any proper market research, I didn't spend ages talking to potential customers nor run in-depth customer interviews…

We just built a project and launched it because that was something WE wanted. WE knew that if it was helpful to us, it would be helpful to others. The worst-case scenario that could have happened is that no one except us would use it. But with the time it would save me, it was already worth it!

When we launched lempod officially, we realized that other people had the exact same need or saw value in what we built. After 2 and a half months in Beta, we decided to start charging for that "side project". 18 months after the launch, lempod was making $600,000 in ARR with very few resources invested.

Such success stories can't always be reproduced and that's mainly because of the different types of Minimal Viable Products that we will investigate below.

The two types of MVPs

According to Reid Hoffman's (LinkedIn co-founder): "**If you are not embarrassed by the first version of your product, you've launched too late**." This is still very true in my opinion.

However, what I've learned from launching two SaaS products is that the level of embarrassment should vary depending on the market you're launching your product into.

Launching in a crowded market

With lemlist, I think we launched our product to the public too soon.

You see, we were in an extremely crowded market. This means that we knew that they were already solutions on the market for the problem we wanted to solve. So, when launching in a crowded market, people will have some expectations regarding your product since they already are used to other products.

Launching publicly exposed us to a lot of people creating accounts and being extremely disappointed with the product. And when people have a bad first experience, it's almost impossible to make them come back…

The thing that we should have done and that some companies are already mastering is creating a private beta. The idea of a private beta is to have people apply to get in. Once you do that you create FOMO[21] so more people will subscribe to the waitlist since they don't want to miss the next BIG thing.

The reason why the private beta is great is that you can filter who you give access to. On top of it, you have the privilege to onboard users manually. This means that every single person who wants to get access to your software will meet with you. It's an amazing way to have a chat with your potential customers and also be fully transparent about your journey and what you're trying to build. By doing so, you can know whether or not the person is the right fit for your product and let them know if that's not the case.

I know that it might sound counterintuitive, but letting people know when they are not a fit for your product, even if they want to get access to it, is something that you should do.

Your #1 priority as a founder is to make sure that every single person who is using your product is getting maximum value with it. If that's not the case, it can generate negative word of mouth and that's something you want to avoid.

On top of it, by being honest and transparent, you actually build trust with the person you onboard and if you remember the chapter about business karma, you know that positive things will always come back to you!

In the early days of lemlist, 99% of our paying customers actually came from demos I made. As a founder, you should be able to sell your beta testers on the vision and not on the existing features. And that's exactly what I did. I spent time explaining why we wanted to create the best sales automation platform on the market and why we wanted to help entrepreneurs build a profitable business. By doing so I also told every beta tester that it was the very beginning of the journey and that we needed their help in building the best product possible.

Something that I've seen that works really well is putting your beta testers in a Slack community, where you'll ask for constant feedback. By doing so you're creating a community from day 1 and you're showing your early adopters that you care about them and that you want to build a product that really helps them.

Now that you know the perfect way to launch a product in a crowded market, you're probably wondering how to launch when you have no competitors?

Launching in an empty market

This is where you should launch as soon as possible. That's what we did with lempod. 2 days to build the MVP and 5 days to get our first 100 users.

The reason why we were able to launch so fast is that no one was solving this problem. So people had 0 expectations from a product standpoint.

Obviously, everyone has ideas of features to develop but their need was so intense that people didn't care about the interface and the extra features. We could have used the private onboarding and waitlist strategy but our goal was to go viral from day 1 in order to reach a critical mass (which we did after a few months). Indeed, lempod was a community-based product and we wanted as many people as possible to be able to access it without any barrier.

Another option would be to launch through invite-only access. For example, each user of the private beta has 5 invites. If you want to join you need someone to give you an invite. By doing so, the early adopters are the only ones who can invite people which by definition puts them in a position of power. Doing so makes you leverage two psychological biases:

1. The fear of missing out (FOMO).

If you need to get an invite to start using a software that means that it's exclusive. Hence people feel the need to join. We all want the things that we can't get.

2. The status effect.

The more people talk about it, the more it becomes a need for people to join. So people who already have access and have invites become the gatekeepers. Since everyone wants to become the gatekeeper in order to increase their social status, it pushes virality even more.

By using this system, you can then give extra invites to people who are doing things to advertise about your launch. These power users then become ambassadors and for them, getting more invites increases their social status.

That's exactly how Clubhouse managed to get huge traction in the early days. But not all products can have such traction from day 1, so let's look at other options.

Getting your first customers

I could give you the list of all the acquisition channels that exist and the best hacks to acquire your customers, but that's not the goal of this book nor the goal of this part. I want to be real with you.

The best way to get your first customers is to reach out to your existing audience. Your first customers will be people you've built relationships with. Why? Because to buy something from someone you need to trust them.

When building an audience or network (no matter the size), people you've met with or who follow you for the value you bring them will trust you. If you didn't know me before reading this book, now you have a better idea of who I am.

On top of it, if you apply all the advice I gave in this book to your business and become successful (which I have no doubt about), you'll probably be grateful.

By bringing you value, I know that we're creating a relationship based on trust. So the day when I'll decide to launch a new project, I know that you will be interested in checking it out.

When a relationship based on trust is established, selling something becomes 10 times easier. That's exactly how influencer marketing works. Brands from all over the world pay influencers to tell their audience about one of their products. By doing so, it drives an enormous amount of sales on that specific product simply because people have trust in the person they've been following for months.

The invisible book sales

That's why you should get as close as possible to your potential customers. To build that trust. So learn from the feedback they give you and show them that you care about them. But always remember that the value you provide comes at a certain price. That's why it's extremely important to get them to pay for your product as soon as possible.

As long as you provide value to people and help them become successful, there's nothing wrong with asking for something in return. And since we're talking about this now, I want to ask you for a little favor. Check out the QR code, I have a special video message for you.

You can also ask them to invite their friends or any people that could benefit from the product you built. I know how tough it is to ask the people you build relationships with to pay for your product. I've been there and I felt really bad at first. I became friends with them and asking them to pay for the product was like begging for money. But it's not.

If you put time and effort into building a business, it has a lot of value. So people should pay for it. You might want to give some discounts at first, but make sure to have people pay for it. That's literally the best support and market validation you can get so make sure to ask for it!

In my opinion, that's the best way to get started and finally put you in a phase where you can grow your SaaS business!

The launch booster - doing lifetime deals?

1 day after launching our private beta we got contacted by someone from Appsumo to promote lemlist in their community.

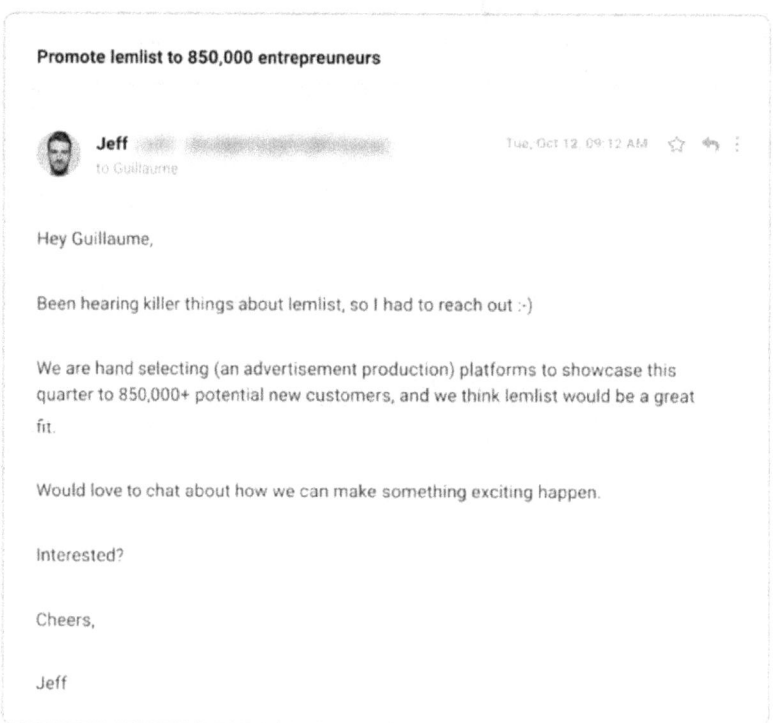

If you don't know Appsumo, it's a huge community of entrepreneurs & small business owners. The platform works as a group buying service and the goal of Appsumo is to offer its community exclusive lifetime deals at a very affordable price.

For every SaaS owner, a lifetime deal might sound like something crazy because instead of selling your software on a monthly subscription, you're gonna sell it as a one-time fee. Let's dive into this idea a bit more.

The pros of doing a lifetime deal

The first thing to look at is the exposure you get from such a big community.

If when you get started you don't have a strong community and audience, then, having the chance to have your software promoted to hundreds of thousands of people is huge.

On top of it, it's a great way to get some cash really quickly and validate your business idea.

Having potentially thousands of customers in two weeks is an amazing way to gather tons of feedback to build the best product ever. On top of it, Appsumo has a kick-a** marketing team that will help you craft the perfect copy for your software and work on your value proposition.

If you don't have the resources to pay a marketing team at that point in time it's also pretty cool to have access to such a talented pool of people for free.

With all these pros, what are the reasons for not doing it?

The cons of doing a lifetime deal

The "lifetime" part is a bit scary. It means that you'll have to provide customer support to all these users for life even though they only paid a one-time fee when your actual customers are paying on a monthly basis. On top of it, people who pay for a lifetime deal don't see the real value in your product as you discounted its price way too much in the first place. Hence, the probability of upselling these users to a monthly paid plan is very low.

Another really annoying part of this is the "black market". There is a huge community of people reselling their lifetime licenses to others in order to make more money as the software gets more and more traction.

But that's not it, people who pay for lifetime deals are usually not the ones you want to target in the future. So, their feedback is sometimes off compared to people who would pay monthly.

However, a lot of Appsumo users are really cool entrepreneurs and founders who can provide good feedback.

That's why when we first got started with lemlist, we thought that it would be a great way to get feedback and build a community with only the coolest users. So we decided to go for it 3 months after launching our beta.

How much money should you expect with an Appsumo launch?

During the launch, Appsumo gave us access to a pretty simple sales dashboard to track the number of Sales/Refunds we had each day.

lemlist (Feb. 2018)
https://appsumo.com/lemlist-recap/

Date	Sales	Refunds	Total
2018-03-15	87	0	87
2018-03-14	197	0	197
2018-03-13	491	0	491
2018-03-12	246	1	245
2018-03-11	83	2	81
2018-03-10	81	0	81
2018-03-09	104	7	97
2018-03-08	125	6	119
2018-03-07	129	1	128
2018-03-06	238	11	227
2018-03-05	535	22	513
2018-03-04	190	5	185
2018-03-03	97	5	92
2018-03-02	131	2	129
2018-03-01	177	9	168
2018-02-28	193	11	182
2018-04-27	254	17	237
2018-04-26	80	9	71

I know that you probably started to take out your calculator so don't worry, here's the recap at the end of the 14-day campaign:
- 3304 new users

- $161,896 in Sales

And that was only 3 months after we started to work on lemlist… you might think that's a ton of money for a 2-week launch. True. But the deal with Appsumo is that they take 70% of the total sales. So we ended up with about $50k which is also a lot of money for a 2-week launch. In order to get a better picture of how it works, let's dive into the process.

The Appsumo launch

Before the launch

We had the chance to work with the Appsumo team on the marketing copy. It was really great added value for us since their marketing team is pretty awesome! Once we all agreed on the copy, here was the following plan for the launch:

Day 1: Publish the deal on their platform with no advertising to their community

Day 7: Send the first newsletter to the Appsumo community

Based on the result of the first newsletter, the Appsumo team will decide whether or not to send a second newsletter

Day 14: Send the second newsletter to their entire community to announce that the deal will end in less than 24 hours

During the launch

As of the first day, we started having a lot of new users. It was really amazing to see all the engagement it generated!

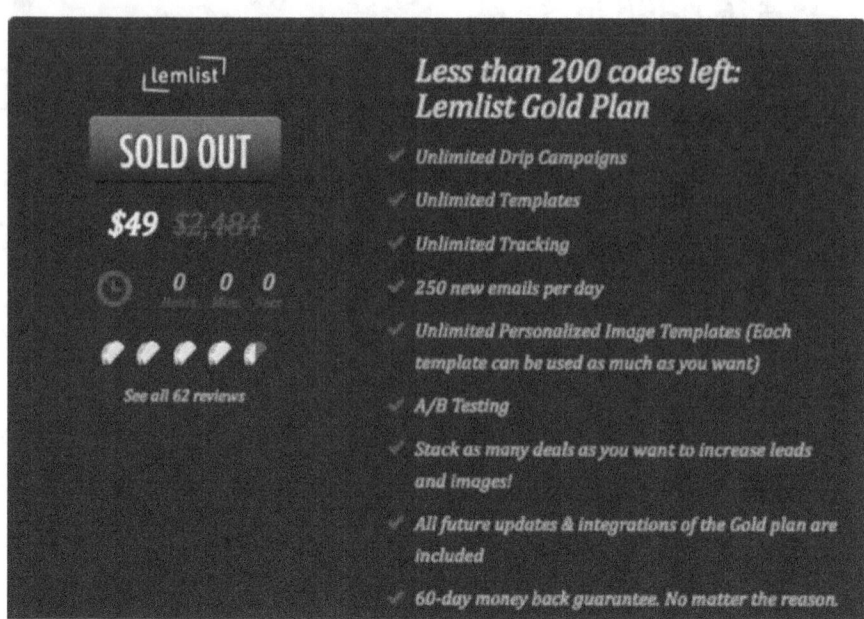

Almost 2000 shares on social networks, 62 reviews with an average score of 4.9/5, and 674 questions on Appsumo!

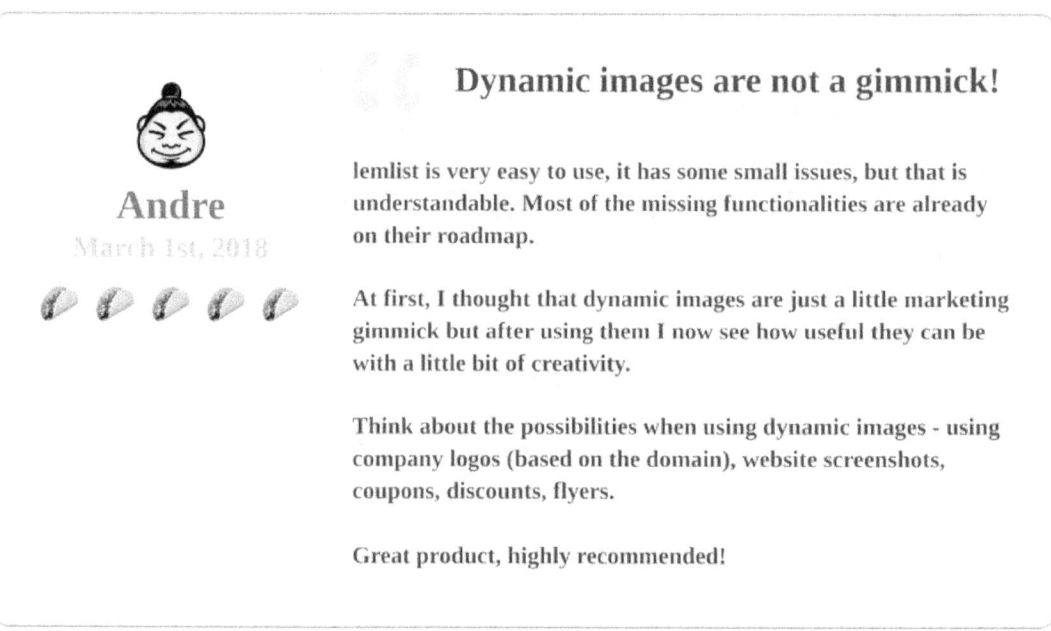

We even had people create review videos about lemlist and some tutorials on how to use it.

We spent 2 weeks, day and night talking with our users. In total we had 1405 conversations that led to tons of learnings and feedback about what we could improve over the following months.

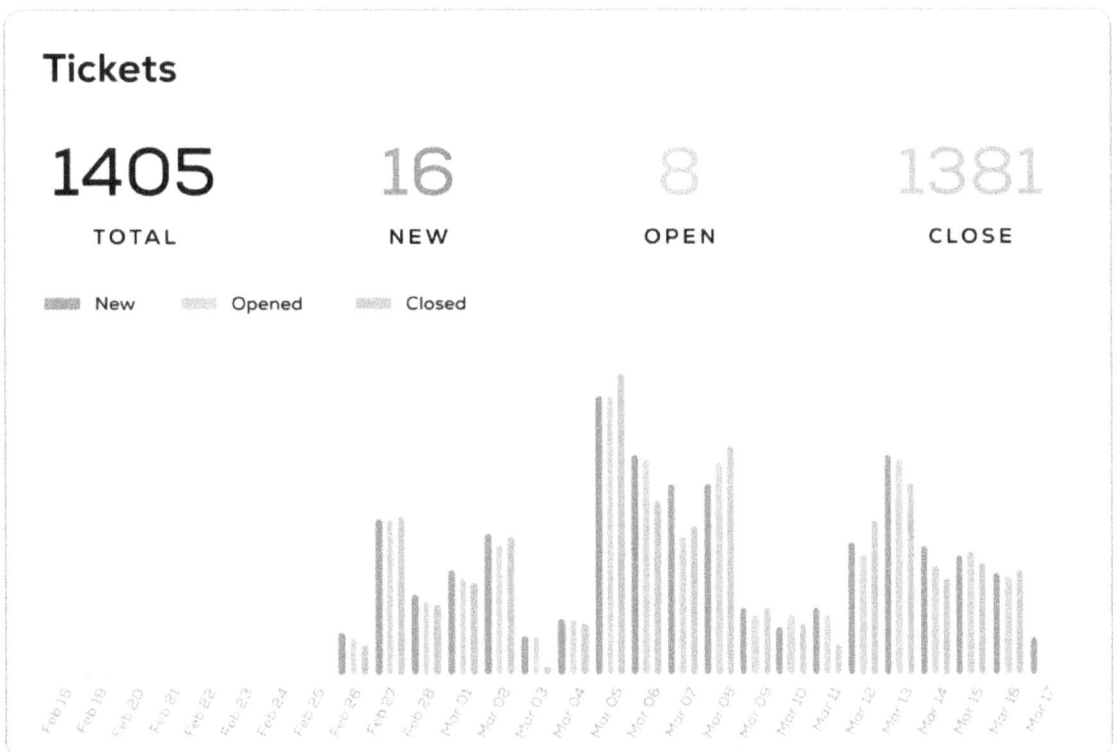

The Appsumo launch gave us a really nice boost and I felt like all the discussions we had really helped us to understand the pain points of our audience 100x better.

We quickly realized that people were struggling to be creative with sales prospecting and didn't know about the technical aspect of it. We launched a community right after the launch in order to provide as much help as possible and create top content. For us, it really felt like getting this huge amount of exposure from the start was a great emotional booster. We finally had proof that people would pay for our software. But they had only paid for a lifetime deal, so we needed real validation.

One week after the Appsumo launch, we decided to put a paywall in place for people to start purchasing lemlist on a monthly basis. I was so stressed that no one would pay…but on our first day, I reached out to 10 of our most active users and they all converted into paying customers!

Seeing these first dollars as monthly recurring revenue was a feeling that I will never forget. We had finally validated that people will pay for what we built. We had a REAL business.

That's when you need to switch to gear #2 and grow your business!

Key learnings

- Making something YOU really want is the best way to get started with a side-project and eventually to start a profitable business!
- The best way to get your first customers is to reach out to your existing audience.
- Building an audience and network (no matter the size) will create trust from the start.
- Creating a private beta is a great thing to master for entrepreneurs.
- Depending on which kind of market you are going into you need to adapt your MVP. If it's crowded, then people will have an expectation you need to meet. If it's empty, the goal should be to get an MVP out asap and iterate later.
- First customers should come from people you know, but try not to discount your product because it will decrease the value in their eyes.
- Lifetimes deals come with pros and cons, it can definitely work well, but you need to be aware of the cons.

G. o

Once your idea is validated and you finally have the proof that people will pay for your SaaS, you can finally call yourself a real business owner! If you're at that stage, congrats! A lot of people who launch a business don't ever get to that stage.

Truth to be told, once you have a few customers you should be able to get a hundred more customers. You "just" need to convince them.

In the last 3.5 years, we made many mistakes growing our company, and learned a lot!

For us, growing to $1,000,000 in ARR was the phase where we learned the most, as it's probably the most challenging milestone to reach.

In this chapter, I want to share all the things we failed at and reveal the secret strategies we used to grow from the first customers to $1,000,000 in ARR.

3 things we failed at that you should avoid

Think that you know better than your customers. After the AppSumo launch, we decided to start billing people on a monthly basis in order to start growing our MRR (Monthly recurring revenue).

However, we quickly realized that our conversion rate was not as high as expected... we had signups but very few sales...we were focusing on 3 metrics:

1. Number of sign-ups
2. Number of activated users (Number of users who signed up and launch a campaign on lemlist)
3. Number of paid users

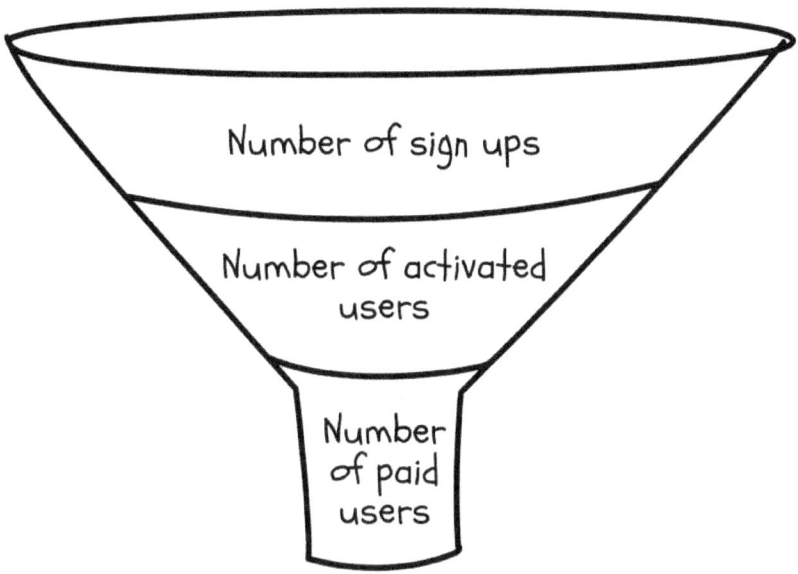

Based on those numbers we made the assumption that if our activation rate was too low it was because our platform was too complicated to use and that people were taking too much time to create campaigns…

So we decided to entirely rebuild the platform without discussing it with our power users. We were convinced that it was the right thing to do, but when I think about it now I realize how stupid it might sound.

We went live and all existing users switched to the new interface…let's just say that some of them were not so pleased about it.

July 12 at 10:07 AM

Guillaume Moubeche at least get a opinion here from your valuable member how's the new ux. Majority members don't like the ux!!! I hope lemlist care about there user feedback. Fb group have nice option for voting.

July 12 at 3:07 PM

Support is saying that the interface changes that were made were due to customer feedback. If anyone of you people suggested this, you're an idiot!

This is the worst UX change I've seen in a LONG time

I LOVED lemlist yesterday, now I can't find anything and I can't update things.

When I saw these messages everywhere in the community, I felt like sh*t…I had failed the community I was trying so hard to serve…I thought that we would lose all our customers.

That's when I decided to hop on calls with all the people who were complaining, while my two co-founders fixed all the different things people were complaining about.

Within 24 hours we had entirely changed the perception people had of the new interface.

> I want to give a shoutout to the lemlist crew for fixing the issues with the new UX while at the same time creating an easier flow to the Campaigns. Honestly, it was a nightmare situation for me and my team when I couldn't access everything.
>
> The lemlist team proved to be helpful and I'm very appreciative of them for listening to their customers. Even when they are pissed..
>
> I'll give them props.. They made it right and long term, I think this will be a better solution.
>
> It was a rough start this morning but I think it's fixed.

After a few weeks of iteration on that new version, we realized that we actually improved our conversion rate from free trial to paid customer by 3x. We also increased our activation rate by 4x and divided by 2 the time it took to create a campaign!

Communicating with your users prior to a huge UX update is really important (duh!) but you should also trust your gut, even when it's a tough call to make.

As a founder, I realized that you should always show up for your customers and not hide from any problems. Even though dealing with a situation like this is never easy. My first feeling was that I wanted to hide under a rock, but my inner self was telling me to show up and deal with it.

I realized that it's during these tough times that you can also build the strongest relationships with your customers and turn "haters" into super fans.

Looking at our revenue growth back in the days, I thought that we could make much more money if instead of going after entrepreneurs and startups, we would chase enterprise accounts.

Enterprise deals or "how to lose your freedom in 5 minutes"

Being able to use our product for sales prospecting, I decided to go after some big names at the enterprise level. After one week I had booked meetings with companies like Uber, Facebook, etc. This is where the fun begins…or not…

I spent 3 months doing between 4 to 9 meetings for each enterprise company I had booked meetings with. Every meeting leads to the next one as you go up the chain of command. And then comes the pilot phase. Awesome you might think! Well, not really…

Working with enterprise-level clients requires a lot of custom work and paperwork. And when I say "a lot" I mean a sh*t ton of work. You need an entire department to handle the legal aspect, and hire another 10 people to entirely change your tech department to meet their requirements.

During 4 months I went from being super excited to work with the most famous companies in the world to "this deal will transform our company entirely and we'll have to start doing custom everything".

Losing my freedom and flexibility quickly became a no-go.

The issue here is, with all these meetings I thought that they would adapt to our standards. That they understood from the start that we were a startup and that we couldn't comply with all their needs. But it doesn't work like this. It's actually the other way around even though the people you meet working at these companies tell you otherwise.

The bottleneck often comes from the legal department. It doesn't matter if everyone is excited to use your product, if you don't comply with their legal requirements or try to negotiate it will never work out.

To give you an example, we had enterprise companies asking us to specifically have all our employee's computers locked down in the office after they end their day. Knowing that we're a remote company, it's impossible to comply with that...

If you want to target enterprise accounts, do it. But make sure to know that you need a lot of time and effort to make things work. It won't be quick.

I was attracted to the BIG names thinking that it would be an amazing way to grow faster, but instead, I should have been 100% focused on our target market (startups, SMBs).

The pitfalls of launching an affiliate program

The essence of affiliation is that if someone is bringing you some new business then they get a commission in exchange.

If you get money thanks to your partners, they get money as well. Sounds fair right? In our case, we decided to give a 30% revenue share to all the people who were bringing some new customers.

At first, the affiliate program was a failure…but at some point, when our growth started to be significant I started to see great traction from our affiliate program...I was pumped! But then I discovered something that would change my view of affiliation...

I was taking a holiday in Sri Lanka and, out of curiosity, decided to search for "lemlist" on Google to see what type of results we would get in this country. That's when I saw a sponsored link as the first search result...I knew we were not running ads though, so this triggered my curiosity. After clicking on the link I realized that one of our partners was actually buying our name on Adwords. Essentially, he was "stealing" most of our organic traffic that way...

Facing this issue I decided to investigate all of our most successful partners and I realized that 2 of them were bidding on our name on Adwords. Others were creating different accounts via their affiliate link to get what would be equivalent to a 30% discount. What I thought was a great acquisition channel became a total failure...

I decided to put an end to that program as I really didn't want to spend time checking each and every one of our partners to know whether or not they've been cheating the system...I feel like we were unlucky on that part as I know tons of people who are running successful affiliate programs. I just think that you need to choose the partners you want to work with carefully.

Moving on from our failures, I want to talk about the things we shouldn't have done!

4 things we shouldn't have done that made us successful

During my journey as an entrepreneur, I received 100s of pieces of advice from entrepreneurs, investors, thought leaders, friends, and family...

Some advice could have been the key to our success. Others would have made us fail. So how do you choose?

I feel like it's important to remember why you become an entrepreneur in the first place.

> To me, being an entrepreneur is about freedom.
>
> – Guillaume Moubeche

So when I get advice from people I always think about what "I" really want to do. In this section, I want to discuss 4 things that we shouldn't have done but that made us successful.

1. You shouldn't work on multiple acquisition channels - focus on one

"G. you don't have a lot of resources or time - you should focus on the single acquisition channel you master and go all in so you're sure to get the best ROI possible overtime" - Anonymous mentor

Everyone will tell you to focus on the acquisition channel that you master. To me, doing one single thing is boring. And let's face it, I didn't start a business to get bored…from the early days of lemlist I worked on multiple acquisition channels that didn't require me to spend money (#CheapFrenchBastard)

The more acquisition channels I was testing, the better our growth was. Each acquisition channel gave me an edge on the next one. And all of these channels connected with each other helped us grow. That's why I call it the growing circle of love.

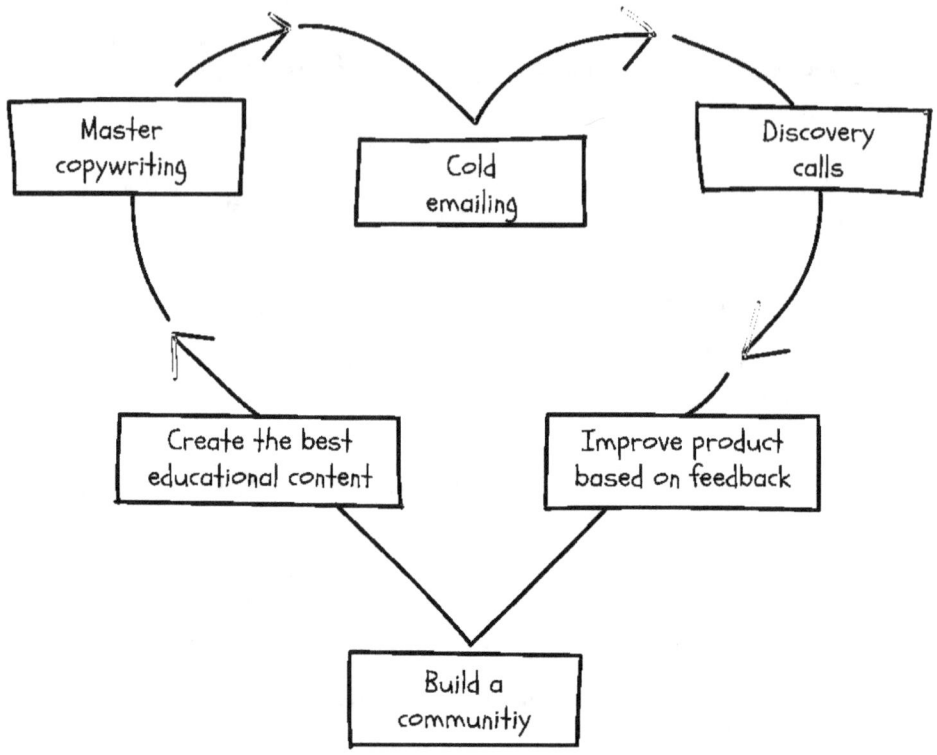

Let me explain. I started sending cold emails because I was really good at it. During my discovery calls, I realized that people were always struggling with the same topics. So I decided to build a community in order to help more of our customers at scale.

The community brought us:

1. Feedback from our users so we could make the best product possible.

2. Ideas to create the most actionable content possible.

We wrote articles based on the topics discussed in the community and then mentioned the community in the articles. Which ended up in people reading the articles and wanting to join the community.

Once I wrote the content I would share it with the community, which boosted the traffic of the articles and the shares.

As our reputation started to grow we got more and more backlinks, increasing our SEO and enabling our articles to rank on the first page of Google. This in turn led to more people finding the articles on their own, and again increased the size of our community.

We wanted to be able to share high-quality content on another vertical, so I started writing posts on LinkedIn. After a few months, my posts were reaching hundreds of thousands of people each month, which dramatically increased my cold email reply rate because people had seen my LinkedIn posts.

Once I mastered each acquisition channel, I was able to hire the right people to continue working on them. As I always say:

> To master something, teach it.
>
> – Guillaume Moubeche

That's what I did with my team, and what my team does with our customers.

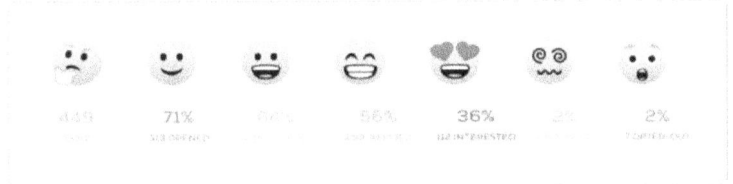

Our team's cold email campaigns are rock solid.

Our LinkedIn posts are reaching millions of people each month.

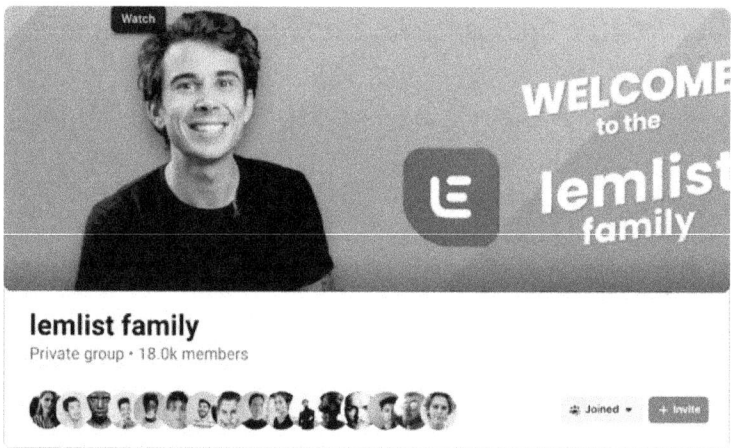

We built the biggest community ever created around sales automation.

Testing all these acquisition channels at the same time made us want to test something that we "shouldn't" have tested.

2. You shouldn't work on multiple projects - focus on one

"Growing one company at a time is really tough. But growing two is suicide." Anonymous VC.

I remember these exact words from an investor I met when we launched lempod back in 2019. 18 months after starting lempod and growing that project to more than $600,000 in ARR, it got acquired.

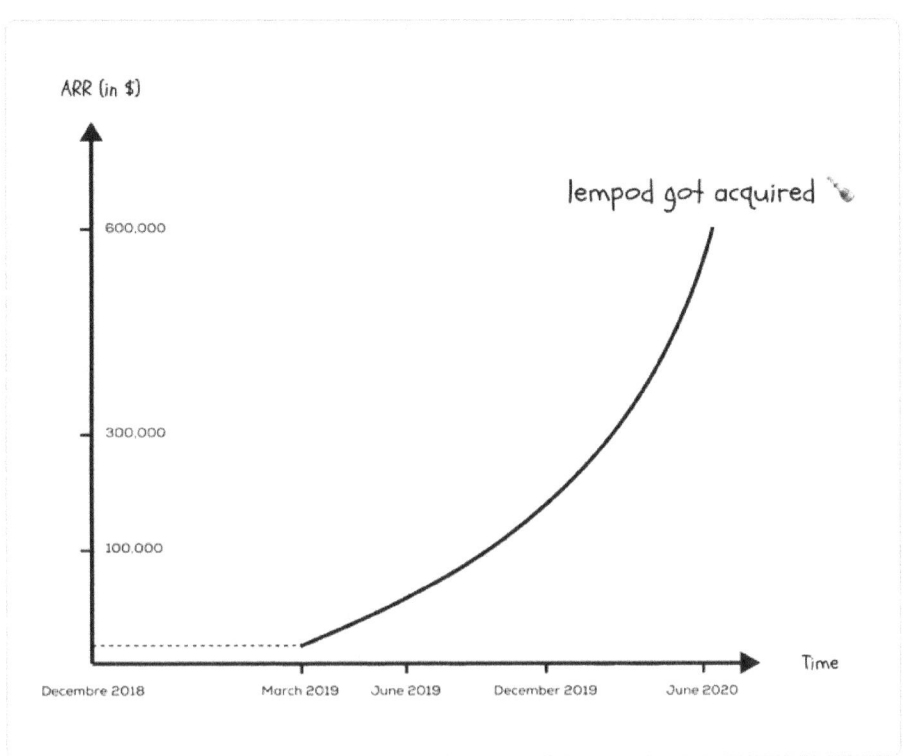

Since our goal with lemlist is to build the first French bootstrapped unicorn, we felt like we needed to be 100% focused.

During that time of managing both lemlist and lempod I learned three things:

1. When growing a business, the success of your users should be your only focus
2. Constraints force creativity
3. Getting acquired is a full-time job (but we'll discuss that in the last chapter)

Working on two projects at the same time was a great way for us to distance ourselves from lemlist a little bit in order to see the bigger picture. On top of it, we also tried to implement new things at lempod and if it worked we would also implement them at lemlist.

Having these 2 SaaS projects forced us to think twice before each action, so we were sure that everything we did was ROI-driven.

Getting a second stream of income is also a great way to mitigate the risk. But when we got an offer we couldn't refuse, we thought that being focused on lemlist would be a smart move!

3. You shouldn't hire people with no track record after crossing $1m ARR

"Guillaume, if you want to keep the same growth rate, you need to hire people with a proven track record after you cross $1M ARR" - Anonymous successful CEO

On the business side (Marketing, Sales, Customer Support), no one had more than 2 years of experience when I hired them. And 90% of the team didn't have any prior experience in SaaS (Software as a Service).

However, every single person I've hired had the same trait in common: the Grind mindset. This means that they all wanted to learn as many new things as possible in order to become the best version of themselves. As Michael Jordan once said: "If you do the work you get rewarded. There are no shortcuts in life."

When people are eager to learn I feel like there's nothing that can hold them back to reach their full potential. Here are a few examples from our team.

Mina joined our customer support team with no prior experience in SaaS whatsoever. 3 months after joining us, she was a top performer with a 100% satisfaction rate from over 200 customer ratings.

Vuk joined as our 1st employee with no prior experience in growth marketing - a couple of years later he's now our Head of Growth and gets interviewed at international events.

Roxana joined as a creative social media manager with no experience using LinkedIn.

6 months later her posts were reaching more than 2.5 million people and she was helping the whole team to reach millions of people each month.

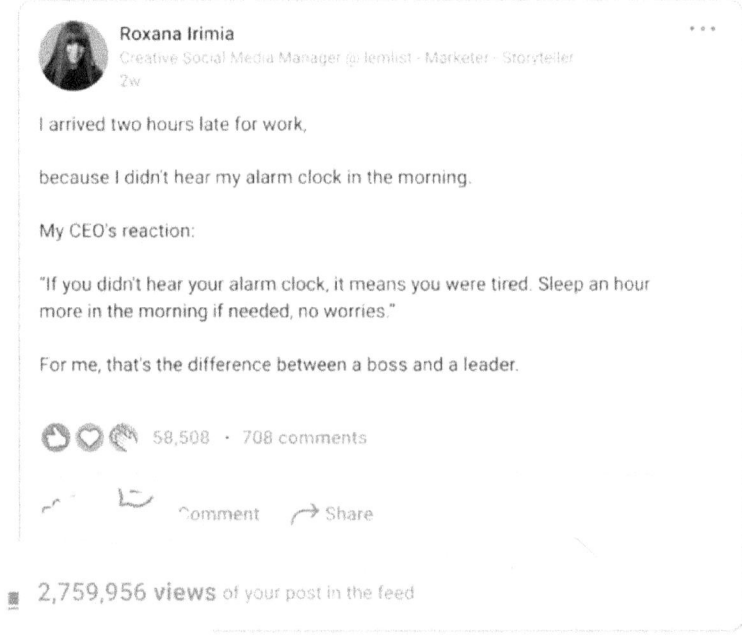

When Simon joined us, he had 500 connections on LinkedIn and his posts were reaching less than a thousand people. Now he has more than 10,500 connections and his posts can reach up to 250,000 people.

Lucille joined us after graduating from her business school and now she's managing our new side project, lemstash.

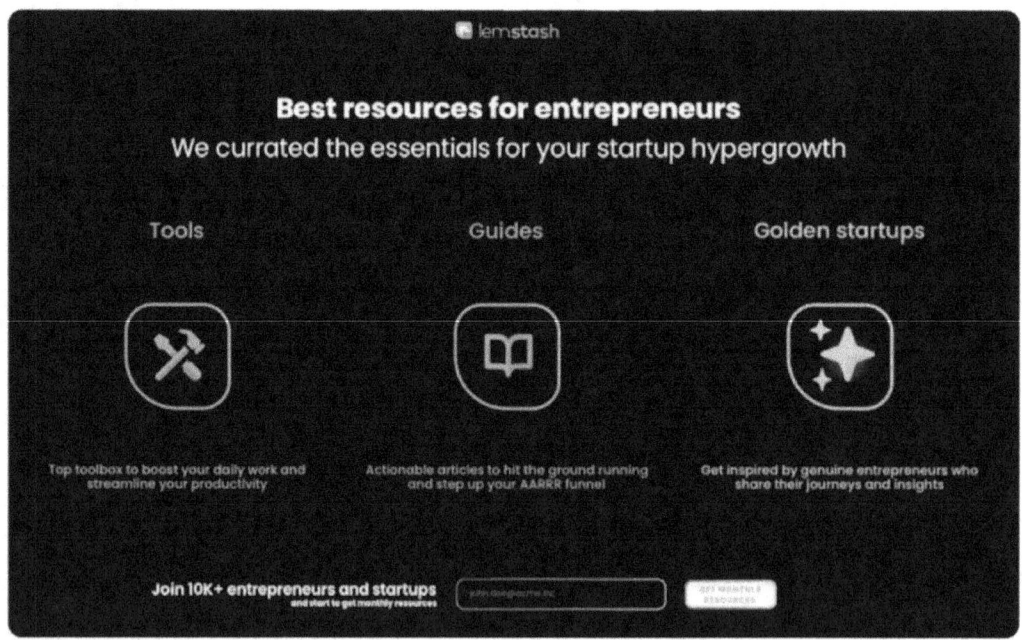

When I started, I had 0 experience in growing a SaaS business. I did everything on my own for the first 18 months. From customer support to sales, and even all of our content marketing. I didn't know every single aspect of how a business should be operated, but I learned.

Our team, on top of being grinders, are all learners and to me, this is 1,000 times more valuable than any track record you can have. Because no matter what problem you're facing, you know that you can find a solution.

> Impossible only means that you haven't found the solution yet
>
> – Henry Ford

4. You shouldn't do things that you can't measure

"If you don't measure each of your actions, how do you know where to double down and where you should stop focusing?" - Anonymous head of growth

There's a huge trend in startup growth teams to be super data-driven. This is good, but often way too over-engineered in my opinion.

> To me, what most businesses and founders lack is not the amount of data they have nor what they can measure. They lack guts!
>
> – Guillaume Moubeche

You can't measure everything in business. It's simply not possible. I really like Tim Soulo's view on the ROI of content marketing.[22] To him, it's impossible to measure the overall ROI of content.

Measuring the few things you can actually track will only be the tip of the iceberg. And for Ahrefs, even if these numbers wouldn't be good, they will not stop creating content because they know that it's working for them. (We're talking about a startup that didn't raise any funding and that is doing $100M in ARR)

I think that measuring everything and trying to see the ROI on every single action you do is definitely reassuring, but most people don't see the hidden costs.

I've seen a lot of startups that are lacking common sense because they think they are measuring everything (which is impossible).

For example, a lot of our content is about giving actionable tips to the community so our users can be more successful. We know deep down that it's working for us.

But how would you measure it precisely? It's not possible. Some things you do impact word of mouth, the activation rate, the retention, etc. But attributing one action to one metric is sometimes impossible.

I prefer focusing 100% on bringing more value to our community and users so they are as successful as possible, rather than spending 100s of thousands of dollars trying to measure everything, knowing that it's impossible.

If your only focus is to make your users/customers successful, there's a 0% chance that you won't succeed over time. And to me, that should be your only focus.

We crossed $10M in ARR in less than 4 years with a team of 35 people and 0 external funding. All of that happened without tracking everything. But it happens thanks to following our common sense and building a growth engine.

Building a growth engine

Essentially, we divided our growth process into 7 pillars.

1. Be kind, build relationships, grow your audience
2. Use your product, use your product, and don't forget to…use your product
3. Write something you would share
4. Sharing love and knowledge everywhere

5. If you want more money, simply ask for more
6. Know your users better than you know yourself
7. Your users should be the hero, you should be their guide

Pillar 1. Be kind, build relationships, grow your audience

Before becoming an entrepreneur, I was convinced of 2 things:

1. To be good in business you have to be a shark.
2. The most successful entrepreneurs are the most serious ones.

I've always been afraid of sharks and loved to have as much fun as possible in everything I do, so I wasn't very into all of this at first... after 5 years of being an entrepreneur, I can tell you that the above is not true at all.

When I started my business I realized that what I liked the most was being able to change people's lives with good advice or a bit of help. With lemlist, I wanted to do that at scale.

That's why, from day 1, we decided to build a community called "lemlist family" on Facebook.

The reason we chose that name is that we consider all lemlisters (people who are part of our community and use lemlist) as part of our family.

Like a family, we wanted to create a safe place for people to share both the fun and difficult parts of doing sales prospecting.

I quickly realized that if we wanted our company to thrive, we had to help more people at scale.

I spent the first 18 months of lemlist talking to our users every single day (weekend included).

With time, I became friends with many lemlisters from all over the world and I realized that the kinder you were, the more grateful people were.

Being super focused on building the best product possible, each piece of feedback we received allowed us to implement a few game-changing features. Let me share two examples of something we started doing to help our users:

Example #1: Landing in everyone's inbox

When sending sales prospecting emails, your deliverability[23] is key.
One of the issues people face when their domain is new is that if they send too many emails too quickly they will end up in spam. To avoid this, they need to "warm-up" their email domain before actually being able to send cold emails.

first name   last name   @   domain   .com

Essentially the warm-up process consists of sending manual emails to friends and increasing the number of emails you send every day so your domain gets recognized by inboxes as something "safe".
One day, one of our power users decided to post something about that exact topic in the community:

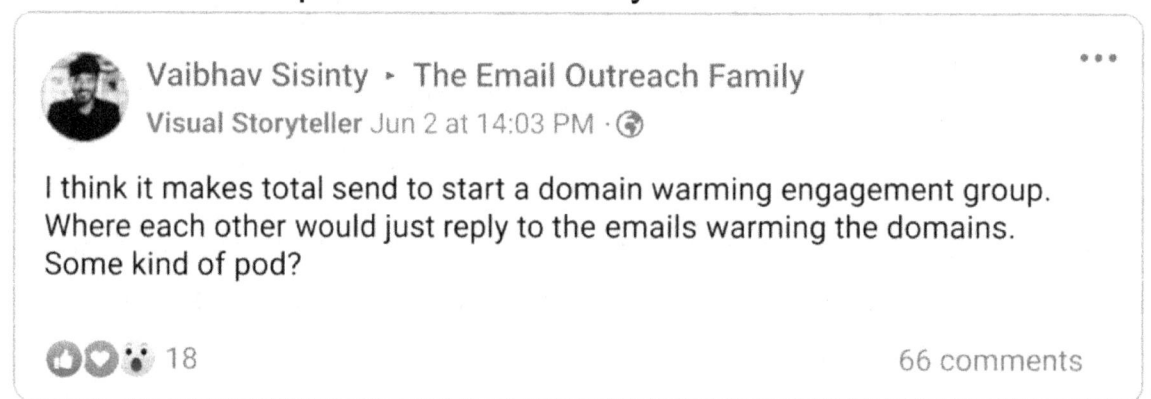

Based on the reactions and comments, we realized that it was a huge pain point for our users. But seeing them doing this manually didn't make sense to me. I knew that we could build a new feature that would allow us to automate this process. So, that's what we did! We decided to have people join a waitlist for that new feature we wanted to develop to do that automatically.
In 24 hours we had 100s of people putting their email addresses on the Google Sheet to have access to that feature.

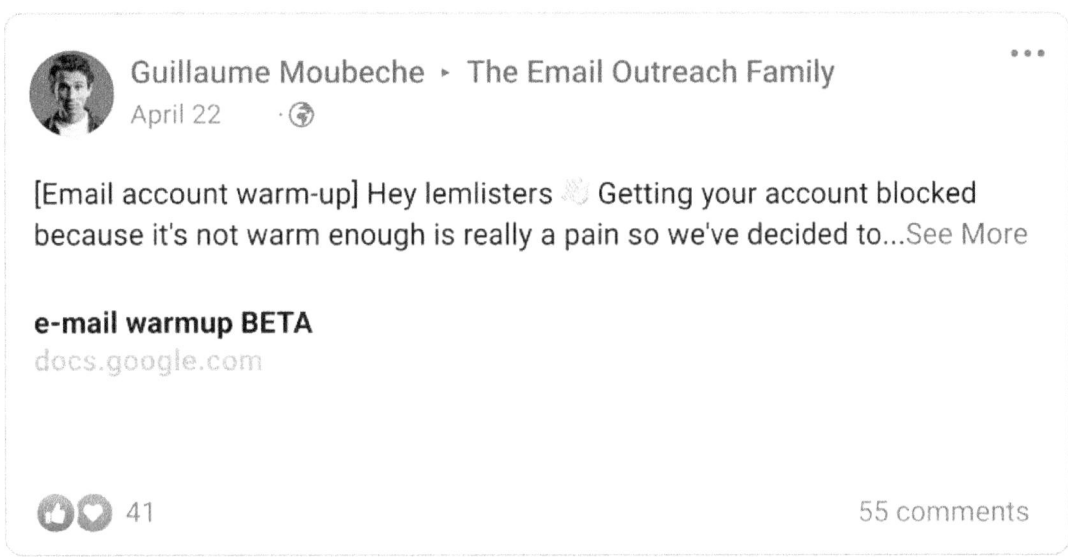

With our tens of thousands of users all over the world, our email warm-up feature would definitely be the best ever created because of the different types of email providers, locations, and domain age from all of the current lemlisters.

On top of it, this feature will be a unique differentiator as it would be based on our user base.

After having my two co-founders put their robot mode ON one more time, we shipped the first version of that new feature after a week and the results were simply amazing. All the comments and reactions we received were super supportive of the new idea.

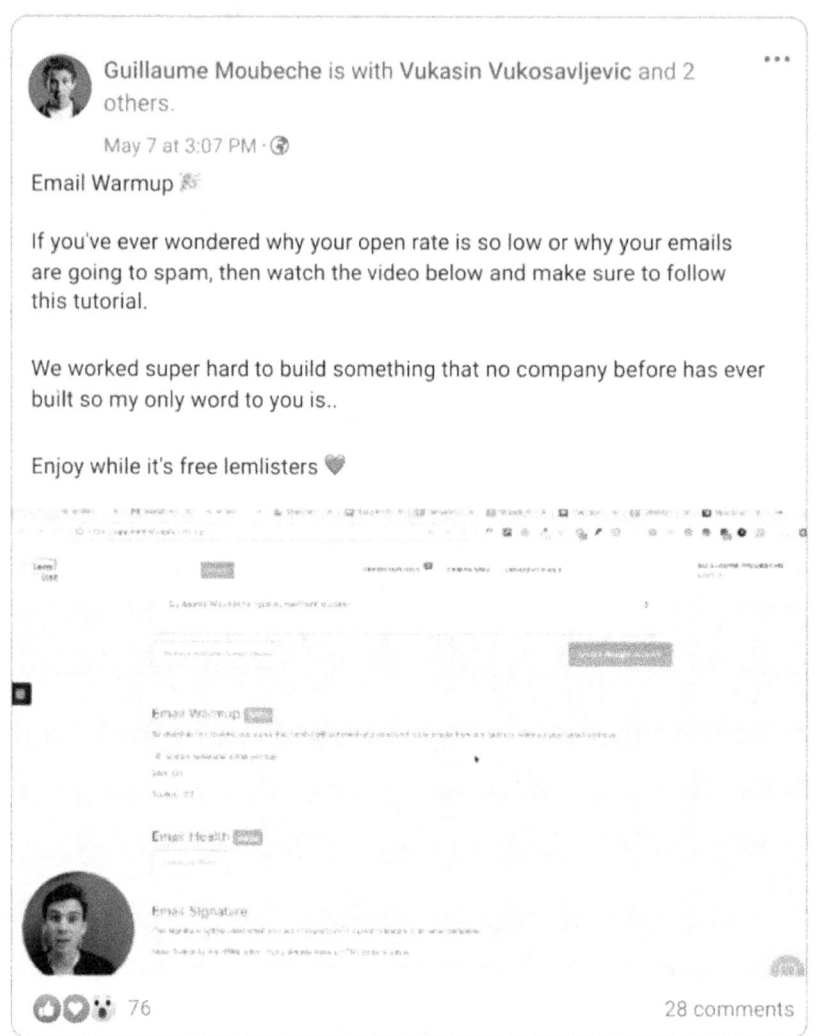

The great thing about building a community is to be able to get feedback instantly about what you're doing. In that case, we managed to tackle a pain that no one in the industry thought of in years…

B. Getting more meetings with your prospects

Using the same user-based approach, we realized that a real pain for most lemlisters was getting more meetings booked with their prospects…

Back then, when you would search "sales prospecting email template" on google, you would always end up on an article sharing templates that were written by content writers who had probably never done a campaign in their life.

Each template being less personalized than the next…and obviously not sharing their results at all…so when people would copy-paste them and send these emails, they would get the worst results ever and, in the end, get discouraged.

With my agency and lemlist, I had done 100s of email campaigns for different industries, so I decided to create one campaign each week where I would share the exact process of writing the email and also the results I got. I wanted people to understand the importance of personalization and illustrate everything I was showing with real results.

At the time, no one would ever share their results, nor the copy of their email, because everyone thought that it was their "secret sauce". I thought the opposite.

My goal is to make sure that more people can connect in the world to build amazing businesses. And to do so, you need to learn how to properly reach out to people you don't know.

link.medium.com
How I got 44 qualified meetings in 1 Day at SaaStr Paris?
Last week, I went to SaaStr Europe in Paris.

One of the articles I wrote was detailing how I got 44 meetings using the right sales prospecting approach. This article got so popular that thousands of people shared it. It was the first time people were actually seeing a fully authentic and transparent article.

On top of sharing the exact template I used and email copy I even shared, how my inbox looked after I sent out this campaign.

	me, **Michiel** 2	**Michiel, let's meet at SaaStr Paris!** - Hi Guillaume, Let's meet each other tomorrow! Let,	15:00 PM
	me, **Maarten** 2	**Maarten, let's meet at SaaStr Paris!** - Hi Guillaume, Thank you for contacting. I've looke..	14:36 PM
	me, **Customer** 2	**Kate, let's meet at SaaStr Paris!** - Hi Guillaume! I love it! Such a clever product. Looking	14:12 PM
	me, **Mads** 2	**Mads, let's meet at SaaStr Paris!** - Looks good - are you at the evening event? tor. 14. ju_	13:05 PM
	me, **Alison** 2	**Alison, let's meet at SaaStr Paris!** - Guillaume, Thank you for reaching out. I will actually	11:18 AM
	me, **Jeremy** 2	**Jeremy, let's meet at SaaStr Paris!** - Question rapide, vous avez utilisé quel logiciel pou..	10:35 AM
	me, **Dan** 2	**Re: thoughts on personalized video?** - I think it is creative and funny, but who are you??	10:03 AM
	me, **Ludovic** 2	**Re: Salesforce Accelerator Program** - Guillaume, see you tomorrow at SaaStr! Hope yo...	9:48 AM
	me, **Lola** 2	**Lola, let's meet at SaaStr Paris!** - Thanks Guillaume, appreciate the video - see you tom	9:25 AM
	me, **John** 2	**John, let's meet at SaaStr Paris!** - Clever ;) John Director · European Operation	8:28 AM
	me, **Katalin** 2	**Katalin, let's meet at SaaStr Paris!** - Hey Guillaume, I appreciate your cold email to me.	7:45 AM
	me, **John** 2	**John P., let's meet at SaaStr Paris!** - Hi Guillaume, Thanks, let's try to meet tomorrow at.	6:05 AM
	me, **Karl** 2	**Karl, let's meet at SaaStr Paris!** - Hi, I am currently travelling on business, returning on t..	4:32 AM

After doing this for about 20 weeks in a row, we decided to launch the biggest cold emailing hub ever created. Every week our top users showcased their campaigns so more people would be inspired to get the same success.

Pillar 2. Use your product, use your product, use your product...

In the previous chapter, I mentioned the importance of building something "YOU" want.

Building a product you need will force you to use it, and the more you use it, the more you'll know what the things are that need to be changed.

On top of it, when talking to customers, you will easily be able to help them with their struggles since you most likely faced the same in the past.

lemlist being a tool for sales prospecting, it was the most economical option to start acquiring customers by using our product.

For lempod, it would boost our reach on social media so it would help us get more inbound leads. Overall using our tools was a freeway for us to acquire customers.

On top of that, every time I was testing something new, and the results were good, I would write an article about it and share it with our community so they could replicate what I did. One of my articles even got featured in a Medium blog with 40K followers.

The more we would detail the step-by-step process of how we used lemlist to achieve great results, the more people would want to do the exact same thing. And if people want to achieve the same results as you, and they see you using "lemlist", they are obviously gonna want to use lemlist as well. It's the same with athletes and the brands they wear.

Using our product and experimenting with new things was also key to building new features.

Based on our assumptions we started to implement personalized videos and landing pages very early in our process.

Since we can generate personalized images based on the person's email address (automatically adding company logo, website screenshots, first name, etc.) we tested this process with a personalized video in an email that lead to a personalized landing page.

Based on some crazy results we had, we decided to implement it for our users and they loved it!

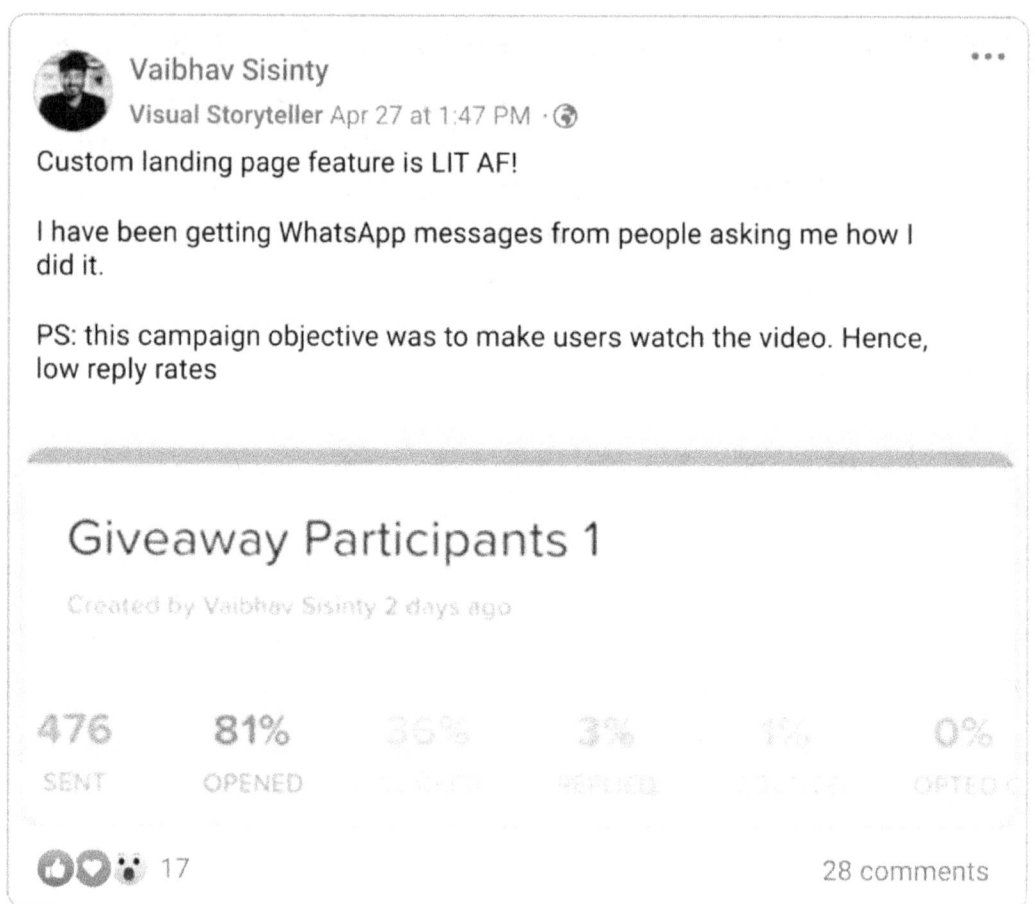

Pillar 3. Write something you would share

When writing content, a lot of people focus on SEO (search engine optimization = how do you make sure that your articles rank #1 on Google for a specific keyword).

However, the articles ranking first on Google are not always the best ones. Sometimes these articles have just been really well optimized for search but don't include enough in-depth information.

When writing content your goal should be for people to share it. That's the best way to know if what you're writing is helpful or not.

On top of it writing content has been key for us for 3 reasons:

1. It was a great way to educate our users on some complex topics such as email deliverability, account warm-up, etc.

2. We were able to write highly valuable and ready-to-use content such as our collection of cold email

templates.

3. Each piece of content was also repurposable on many different channels.

But now you're probably wondering how to find ideas about what to write about… I remember not knowing all the topics I could write about when I first started.

But after spending some time with our users, I had an idea. When a few people were asking me the same questions about something I knew the answer very well, I would write an article answering these exact questions in a very detailed and actionable manner.

Let's take one example here: people were always wondering how to find people's email addresses or even how to get the best deliverability possible.

After spotting these topics we decided to spend some time finding the best keywords to use (using tools like Ahrefs, Ubersuggest, etc.) to be sure that a lot of people were searching for those specific topics.

To keep it simple and don't go too much into details, you can find tools online that will tell you how many people are searching for a specific keyword online - that's called the search volume.

Keyword Overview: barack obama

SEARCH VOLUME	SEO DIFFICULTY	PAID DIFFICULTY
823,000 HIGH	48	1 EASY

Keyword Overview: guillaume moubeche

SEARCH VOLUME	SEO DIFFICULTY	PAID DIFFICULTY
170	18 EASY	1 EASY

We can clearly see that people are much more interested in Barack Obama than in me (which makes sense).

By knowing what people search for, you can create an article that answers all questions people might have about a specific topic. This is usually how you make sure that your article ranks on top of Google search results.

But as always, the focus for us was that the article would be shared by people as much as possible. It had to be super actionable. And that's what we did to help people find anyone's email address on the planet using 11 different methods.

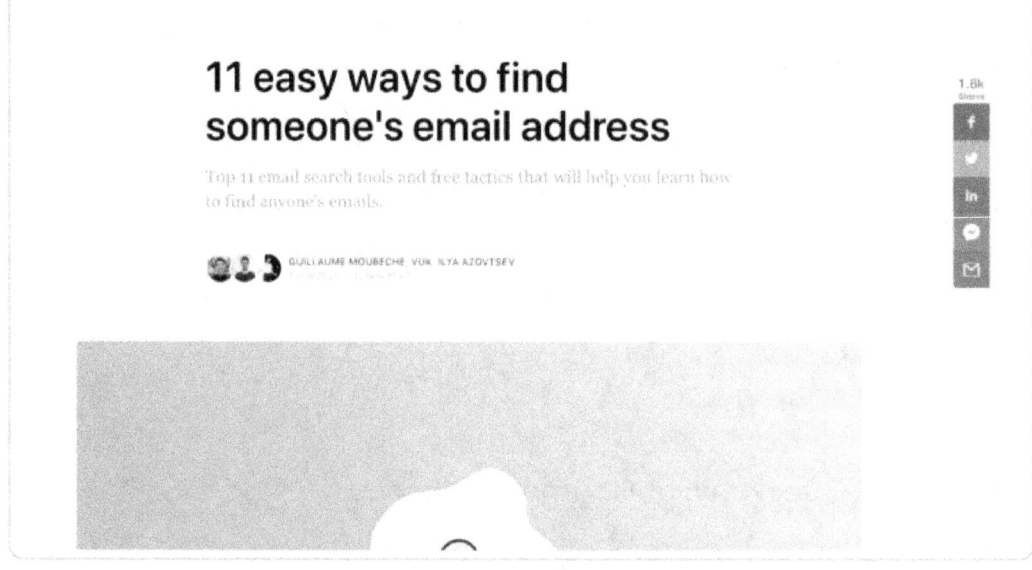

More than 1,600 people shared it.

You're probably wondering why we want to write about such a topic when our tool is much more oriented towards people who are sending sales prospecting campaigns.

Well, people who want to find email addresses for sales prospecting often need a tool to send emails in a personalized way. If we position ourselves as the ones who brought them value by explaining how to find someone's email address, then it becomes obvious to them that the tool used to send these emails should be lemlist!

In every industry, you can find topics that will bring benefit to your users while at the same time positioning yourself as a thought leader. That's also what we did with the deliverability topic. Since our combined users had sent 10s of millions of emails across more than 10,000 accounts, we had a lot of data to know what was working or not. Based on that, we analyzed all the best practices and decided to write another in-depth guide about email deliverability and account warmup.

However, content creation is only 20% of the work…The 80% will come from content distribution and repurposing and that's actually our 4th pillar.

Pillar 4. Sharing love and knowledge everywhere

In the early days, it was just 2 developers and a random French guy (hello, me). However, this content strategy of documenting every single thing we were doing attracted a rising star…Vuk.

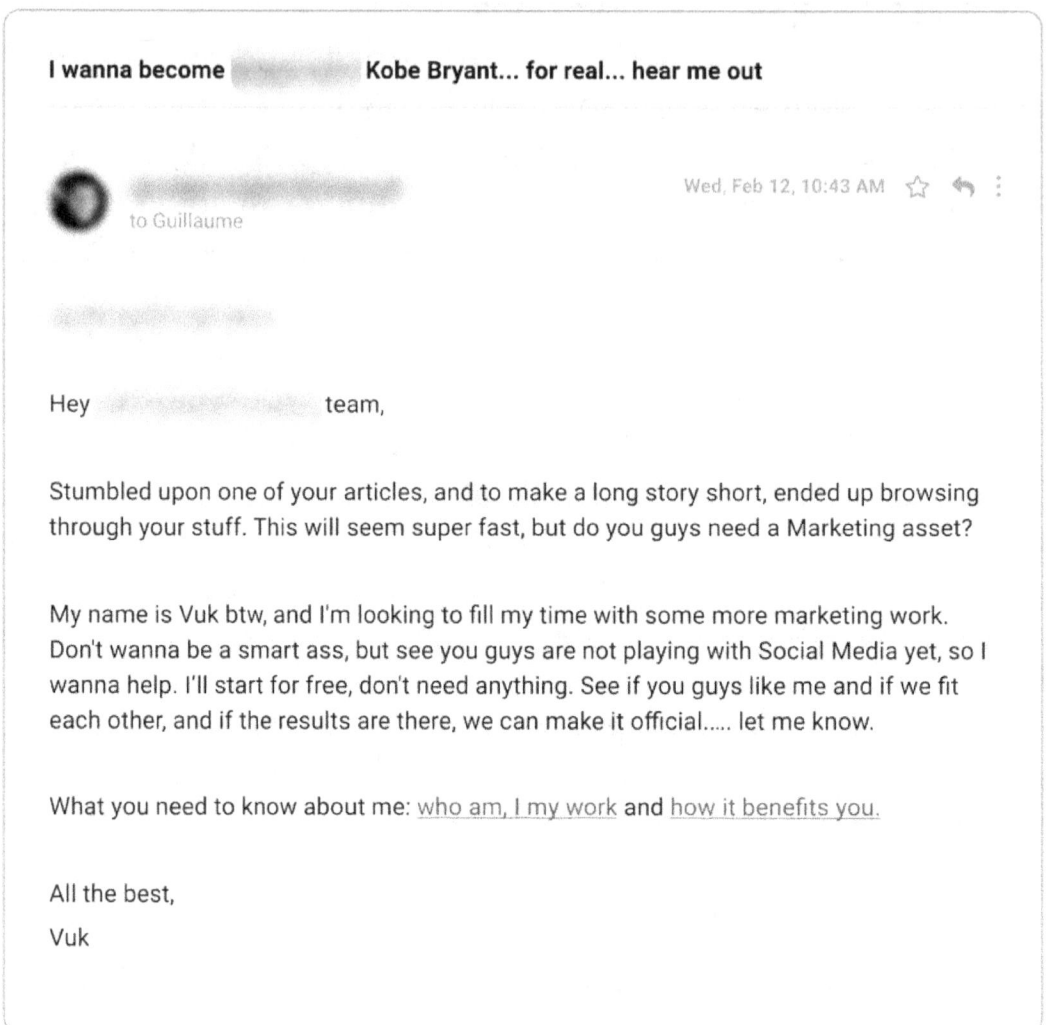

After giving him a shot, Vuk showed me his thirst to strive and I really liked his hustle mindset.

A few months after that we were meeting in Paris to build this 4th pillar. The concept is pretty simple. We're a small team with great ambitions. Being small means that we wouldn't be able to produce hundreds of articles every single month.

However, each article can be repurposed and shared on many different communities or media channels. We divided our strategy into 2 parts:

Part 1. Repurposing content on multiple platforms

This might sound pretty easy, yet most companies forget about it…for example, let's say that you record a video about 10 tips about cold emailing. You can now transform this one video into 10 shorter videos and write posts about it on LinkedIn. That's actually what we did.

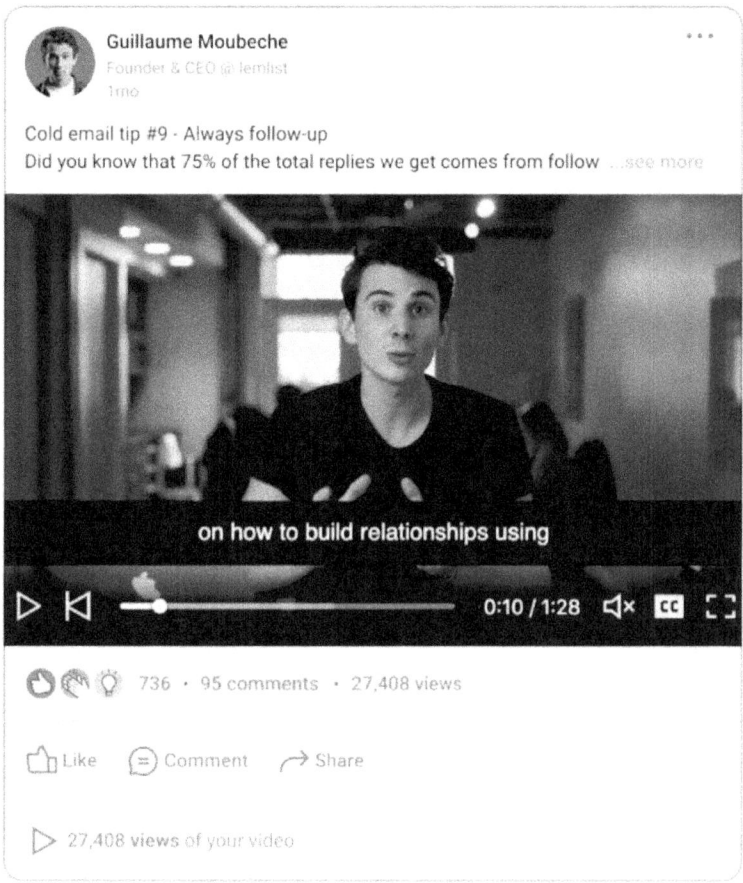

So each week, we would give tips around a specific topic. By dividing one piece of content into smaller pieces you usually make it much more digestible, especially on social platforms, and that's why each of my videos was getting tens of thousands of views.

Another example is when Vuk killed it by repurposing some articles on Quora and answering a lot of questions related to our area of expertise.

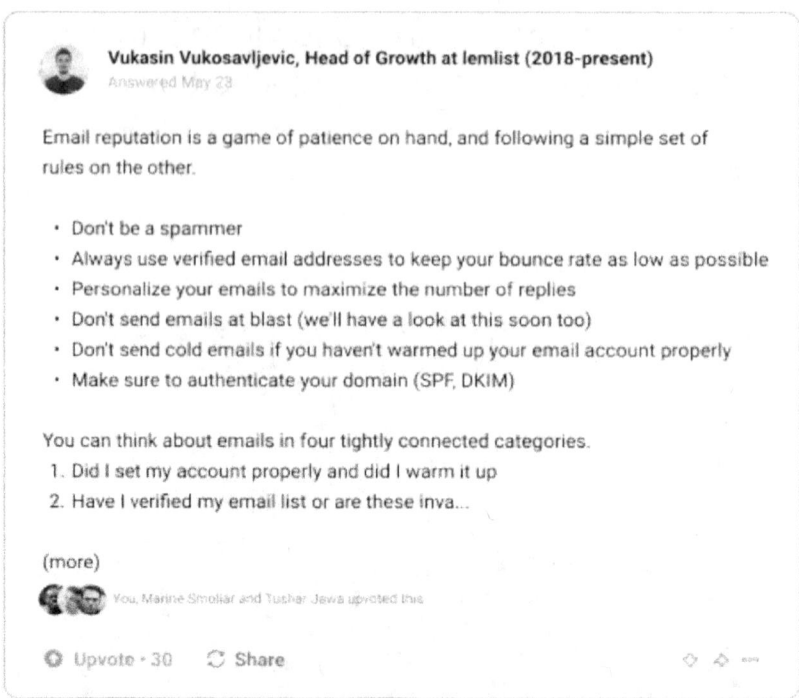

If you don't know Quora, it's basically a social platform where people ask questions. This social media channel is based on the community of people willing to help each other by answering questions people might have.

It's a great way for any business to position yourself as a thought leader on a specific topic by answering people's questions. To do so, you can use the content you wrote in your articles and adapt it.

After repurposing each and every single piece of content, we were able to drive more visitors to our website from various sources and define what was working or not.

Part 2. Sharing content everywhere we could bring value

Once you've written content you need to make sure that it is seen. If you don't do anything about it, it will probably end up being forgotten in the depths of the internet.

The energy you put into content distribution should be at least as important as when you write your content. And to distribute your content you need to find places to share it.

Unfortunately, there is no secret sauce here…you need to spend time searching for where your audience hangs out and then, give them the content they like. It can be on Facebook communities, Slack groups, subreddits or even online forums such as Growth Hackers where we got featured in their newsletter a few times already.

One more time, the creation and distribution of content should be about one single thing: helping people. It's only by writing the best content possible that you will build trust with your audience. The more people trust you, the happier they are to be joining you as customers! This leads us to the next point about pricing.

Pillar 5. If you want more money, simply ask for more

The scariest thing to do as a founder is…increase prices…

If you've been hanging out with entrepreneurs, everyone talks about "price increases" and it sounds pretty magical…

You want to make more money? Well…increase your prices! It's obvious. I even started to recommend increasing prices to many other founders! But when it came to lemlist, I chickened out…

What if people don't want to pay that amount of money? What if people find it too expensive? In the end, it's only a matter of perceived value…

> *A higher price means more value.*
>
> — Guillaume Moubeche

After postponing our price increase for months (yes, I was really that scared) we decided to increase our pricing by 50%. Yup.. 50%... I thought it would be the biggest mistake ever. But guess what? In the end, it was our best month! Our growth rate increased and our conversation rate stayed exactly the same.

Even though you might be scared, make sure to increase your price on a regular basis. As you're adding features to your product, investing in your support team and content, you're ultimately providing more value to people. The more value you provide, the higher your price should be.

Worst case scenario, people are complaining too much about the price changes and you'll go back. That's why it's always important to spend an enormous amount of time with your users - which leads us to pillar #6.

Pillar 6. Know your users better than you know yourself

Being user-centric is something any marketer, founder, or entrepreneur has heard of. People use this word as something magical, yet most people don't put in the effort to be really user-centric.

To me, it's not only about being user-centric. It's about getting to know your users better than yourself! Spend so much time with them that you know exactly what they are struggling with, what their goals are, what they're dreaming about...every single thing that could help you get closer so you could better help them achieve their goals!

To do so, we decided to run some user surveys using lemlist. The goal was to get to know a small segment of our paid users really well to understand what they liked or disliked.

Regarding the survey, we decided to use what Rahul Vora did

for Superhuman, and ask 4 questions:

> 1. How would you feel if you could no longer use lemlist?
>   A. Very disappointed
>   B. Somewhat disappointed
>   C. Not disappointed
>
> 2. What type of people do you think would most benefit from lemlist?
>
> 3. What is the main benefit you receive from lemlist?
>
> 4. How can we improve lemlist for you?
>
> – Guillaume Moubeche

Getting enough replies to a survey is usually a pain so we decided to make it super personalized! And guess what? Almost 60% of the people clicked on the link to answer the survey. Usually, people get an average response rate of around 5-10%. So how did we manage to get so many responses? Let's take a look at our emails:

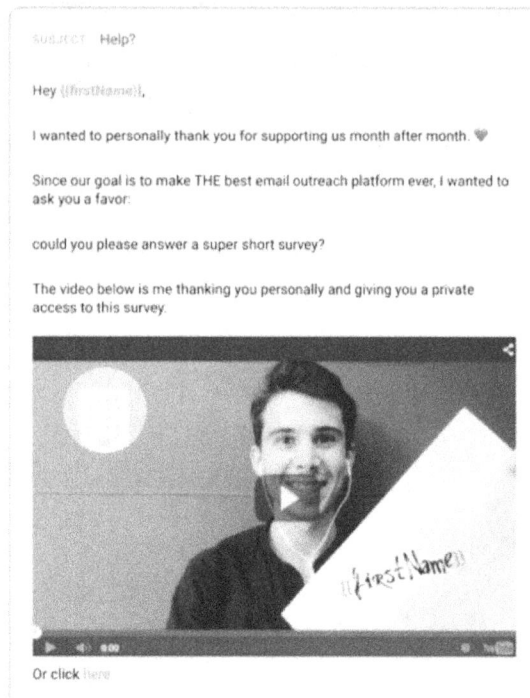 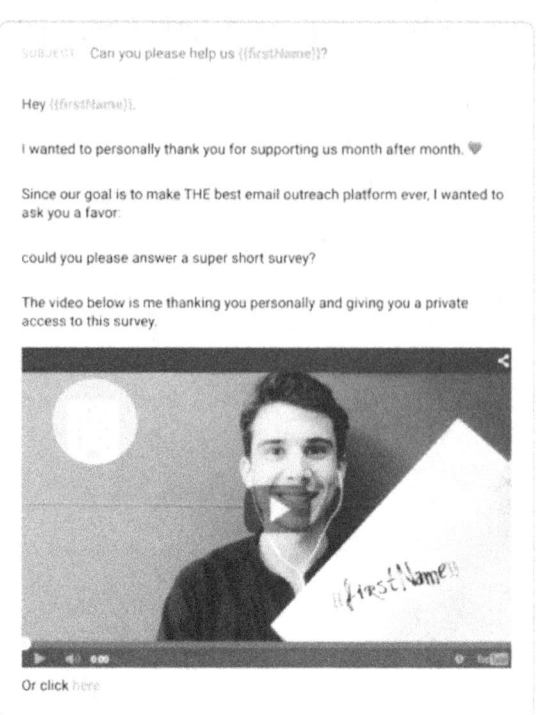

Once our users clicked on the video, they would land on a personalized landing page (think of it as a personalized website) including a survey they could write answers to directly.

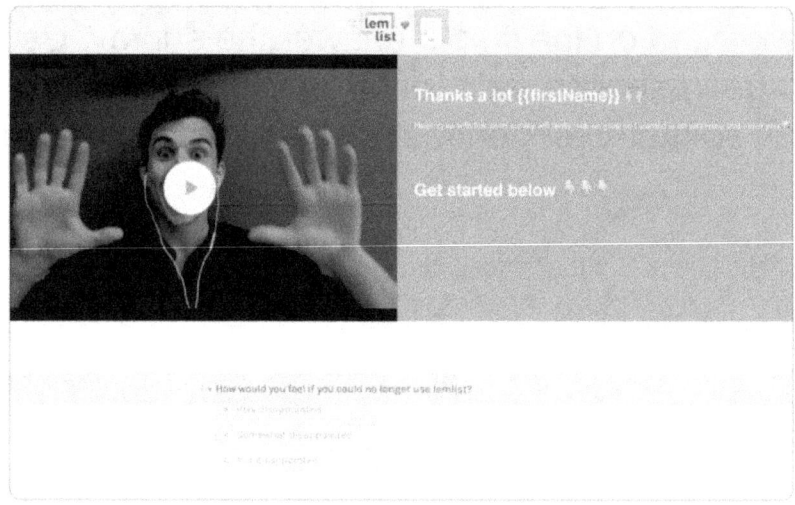

Each landing page was automatically personalized using lemlist technology.

In total, we had almost a 100% conversion rate from clicking on the video to survey completion. It was also a great way to illustrate some of the latest features of lemlist to our users.

In the end, we had the following results to the first question "How would you feel if you could no longer use lemlist?":

54,5%	Somewhat disappointed
43,2%	Very disappointed
2,3%	Not disappointed

Based on those results we were able to really split our customers into buckets and understand two things:

1. Who are those users who would be "very disappointed" if they couldn't use lemlist anymore?

Essentially you want to focus on that segment in order to find more people who will find your product vital. When people find your product vital, you know that you're bringing them enormous value. These people are the ones who will be your super fans and that's why you need to spend extra time with them.

2. Why are some users only "somewhat disappointed"

For that segment, the goal is to understand how you could move them towards bucket number 1 of your power users. Sometimes, just having calls with them will allow you to better understand how your solution can become indispensable to them. It's also important for the CEO to show your users that you care. It will build even more trust and make you stand out.

From all my entrepreneur friends, I know very few who are still spending time with their existing users after crossing their first million in ARR. They think that their time would be better spent doing something else. I disagree.

To me, the most important thing as the CEO of a business is to never lose sight of the reality of what your users are dealing with on a daily basis. Try to stay hands-on as long as possible.

Once we crossed $8M in annual recurring revenue, I even did 100 coaching sessions for our top users. I literally don't know any other CEO at that stage who would spend 50 hours with their users.

I don't say it to brag, but just to show you that doing things that don't scale will make you stand out.

> If you want to be part of the 1% you need to be ready to do the things that 99% of people won't do. Period.
>
> – Guillaume Moubeche

Having such insights was really of huge value to keep getting to know our users even more and making sure to create a unique relationship.

Pillar 7. Your users should be the heroes - you should be their guide

From day 1 at lemlist, our mission has been to empower sales teams from all over the world to book more meetings with their prospects and build meaningful relationships.

To do so, we decided to build the biggest community around sales automation: lemlist family.

In 3.5 years, we grew the community from 0 to 19,000 members. By focusing on helping lemlisters grow their businesses with sales prospecting, we had created a unique way to communicate. Our community allows us to get direct insight on what to focus on for our feature development.

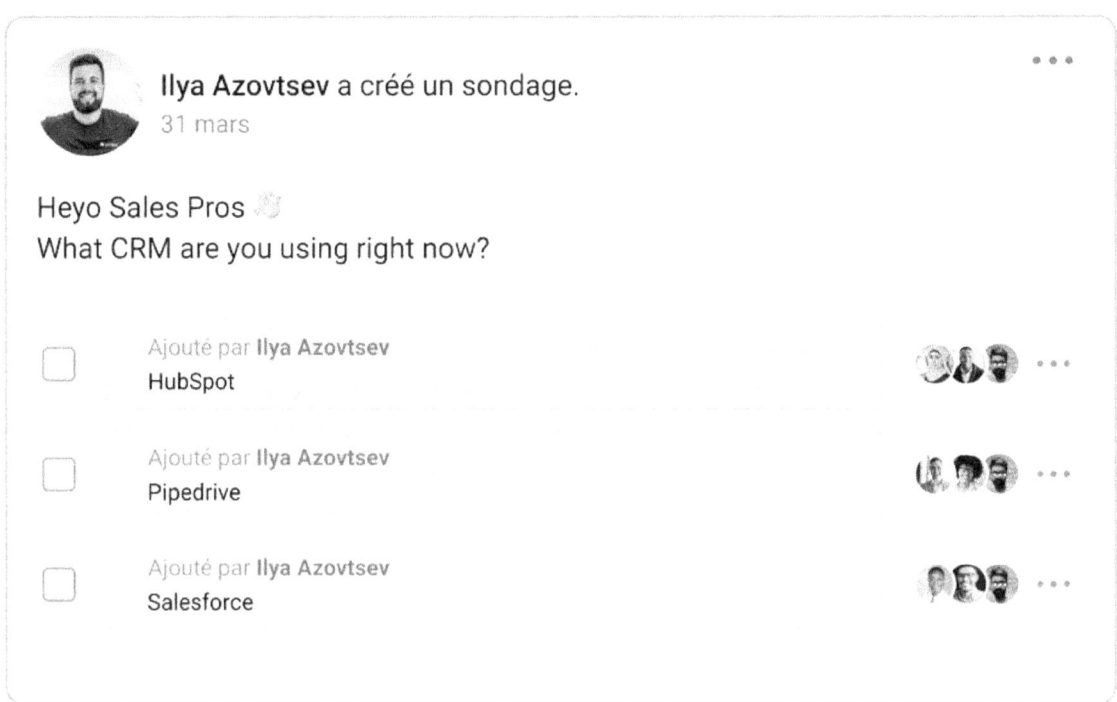

Publishing polls in the community.

All the posts from people would also help us to get tons of insights in order to write the best guides and content possible for our users. But that's not it. By bringing value constantly, people started to help each other as well.

99% of the content in our community is now user-generated content. This means that people will post about their issues and other lemlisters will help them.

By creating this movement of ambitious entrepreneurs who are here to help each other succeed, we created a whole new world. A safe world where it's ok to talk about failures and challenges. A world where people will help each other because they know that being a lemlister means having the ambition to become the best version of yourself to grow a profitable business.

But to build and keep such a high quality community, we had to be very selective from day 1. Both when it comes to the people who join the community but also about the posts people published. No promotion, so spam, no hate - only love and good vibes.

With all these insights from our users we were able to write the most actionable guides, since everyone in the community was happy to share their internal processes. Some of our guides were actually reshared by companies like Pipedrive and gave us even more visibility.

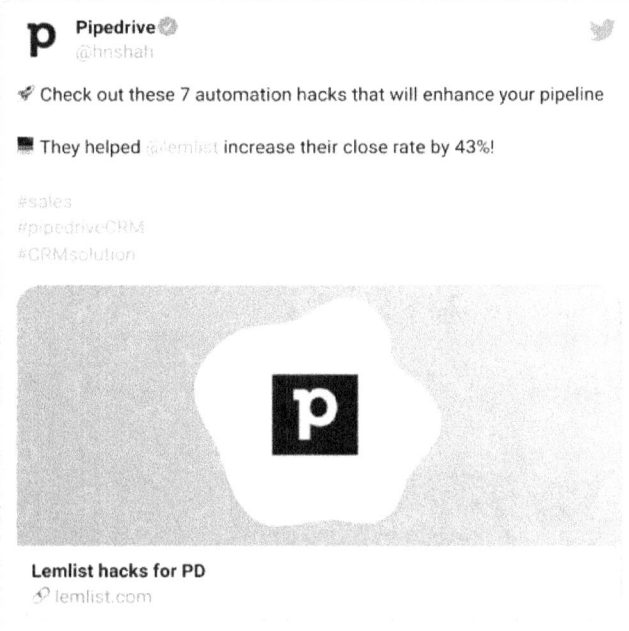

Having Pipedrive sharing our content with their community

Because the power of a community relies on co-creation, we decided to get in touch with the best lemlisters in order to share the best tips and tricks about sales prospecting!

In order to push this co-creation even further, we decided to launch a new type of weekly content called "lemlister of the week".

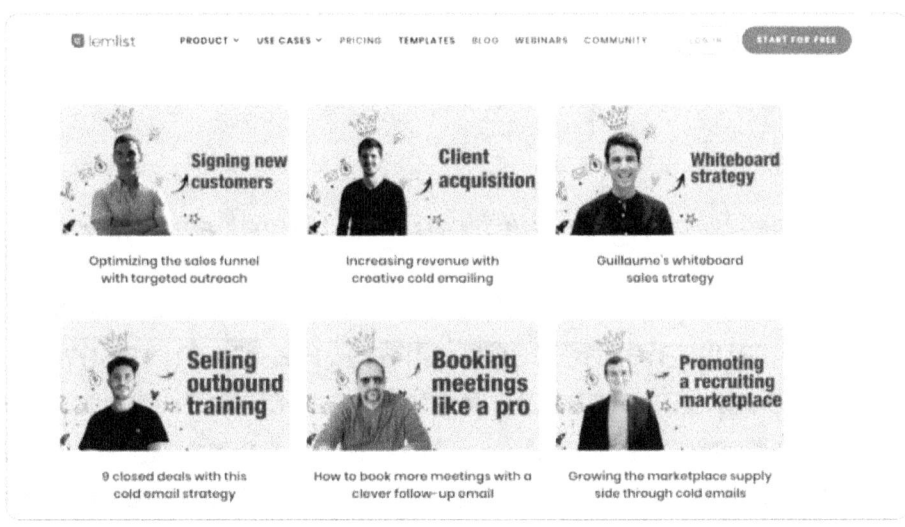

The best campaigns from lemlisters explained

Essentially, each week, we pick a lemlister who had amazing results with his/her sales prospecting campaign and we explain why it worked. From the targeting down to the copy.

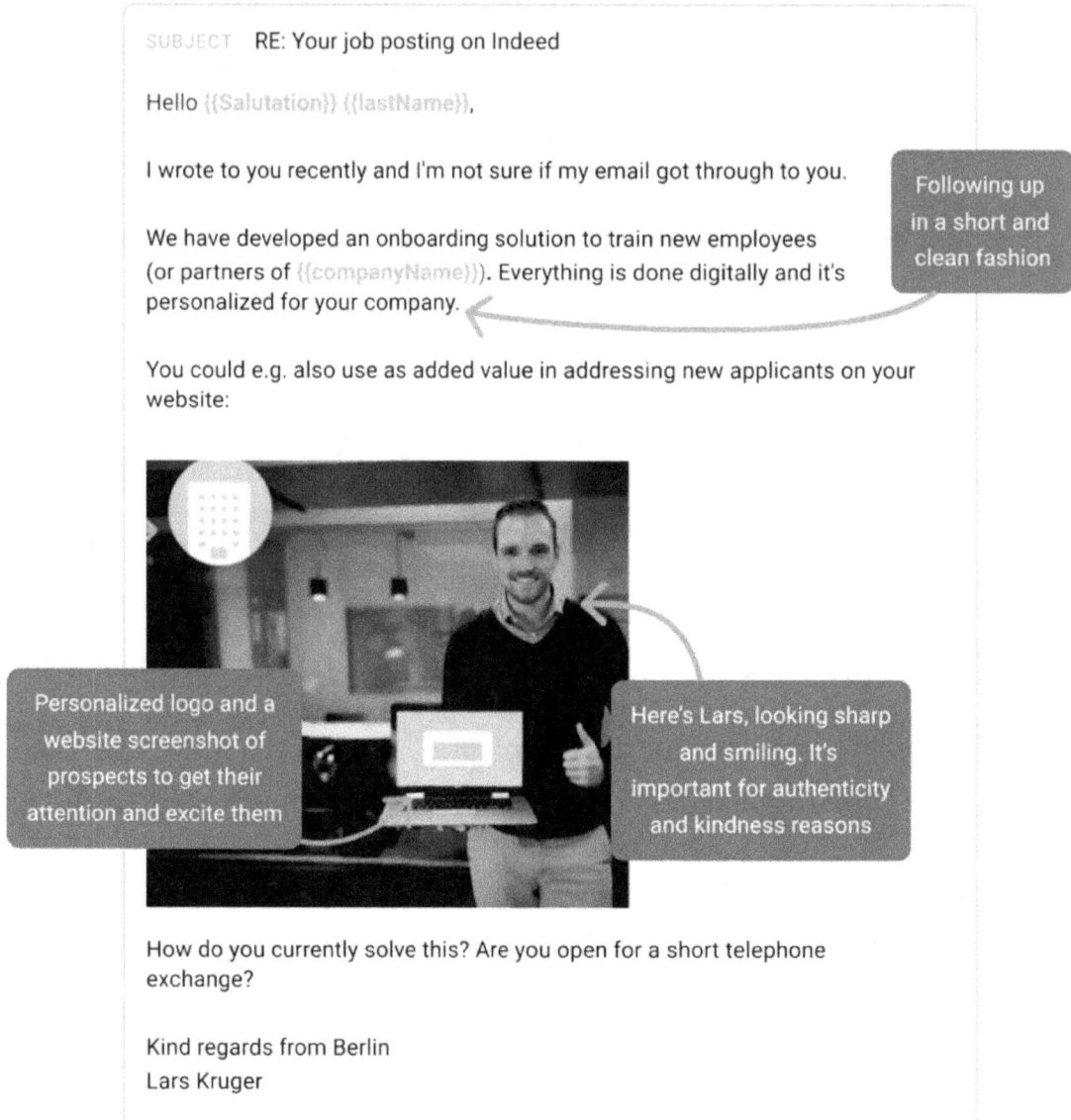

Top-performing email from a lemlister explained

By doing so, people were able to see what other lemlisters were doing in order to replicate the same strategies for themselves.

For us, it's such an amazing way to get closer to our users while at the same time providing a lot of value to our community. And for the "lemlister of the week", it's a great way to get tons of exposure.

On top of that, we even had some really cool and not-so-traditional success stories like when a lemlister decided to send a personalized wedding invite with lemlist, getting a 95% Click-Through Rate.

Post in our community from Juraj who used lemlist for wedding invites

More than just a community, we really consider the lemlist family as our family. Being part of the community is not just about getting help on a specific topic. It's about joining a movement of ambitious individuals.

Being part of a group of really cool people who are ready to spend time helping you if you need help. Because in the end, we know that we're all in this for the long run. That business is a marathon and not a sprint. That business is not always about profit and money. That business is about meeting people worldwide and learning from each other. And ultimately, by creating all these awesome relationships, you will succeed to build a kick-a** business!

Having this awesome vibe in the community, we wanted people to be able to follow our journey. That's why we started what we called "Build in public".

Community first - Building in Public

"I started to build an audience way too soon" - no one ever

I've talked a lot about audience building in this book and why it is so important to build a community even before you actually start your business.

As you'll grow your business, you'll see that the way you build your audience and network will evolve in order to adapt to your business scale and goals, and objectives.

Why build an audience first business?

I can't count the number of influencers who became millionaires almost overnight when they decided to launch their own brand.

We've seen this a lot on Instagram with lifestyle influencers turning into business owners. We can think of Kayla Itsines, a fitness influencer who created a $46M business by launching her own training and nutrition program.

Gary Vee, who is more famous on the business side of things, decided to partner with a shoe brand that also generated millions of dollars.

The more engaged your audience is, the easier it will be for you to launch a successful business. If you're not convinced yet, here are a few reasons why building an audience is literally the best way to grow a business:

- Technology, features, product, etc. CAN be copied - the relationships you build with your audience CAN'T.
- It's an asset that you'll keep forever. If this business doesn't work out for some reason, you'll still have an audience and hence a source of potential customers for your new projects.
- It will make everything easier. The bigger your audience is, the more people will want to do business with you, invite you to speak at events, etc.

How do you build an engaged audience?

For us, the key was helping other people achieve something they can't achieve alone. We wanted to guide them through the process of growing their business and how to be successful at getting in touch with anyone.

Here's how we decided to split our content into 3 different categories.

1. Helping people succeed:

In this category of content, you should focus on what success means for your audience. For lemlist, we know that "success" to our audience means growing their business and acquiring more customers.

So, a lot of my posts were focused on giving the best resources to write good cold emails in order for them to meet with more potential customers.

2. Building in public doesn't always mean bragging in public

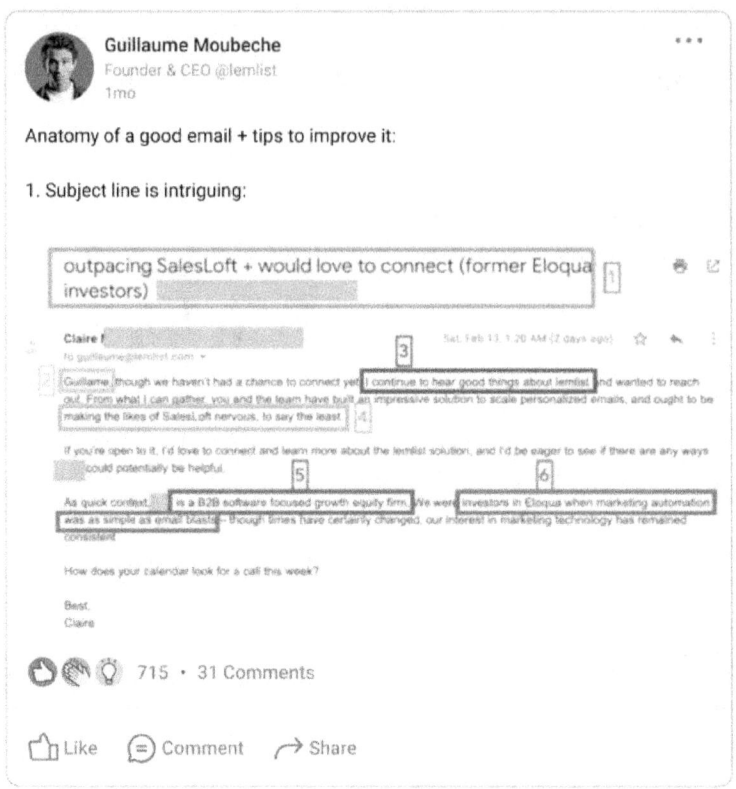

I know that you're probably wondering how the hell to get started with content. How exactly do you find ideas? I've been there.

But to be honest, you just need to get started. The ideas will come afterward. It's the same mechanism as the box story I mentioned earlier.

What's in the box?

Documenting what you do is the easiest way to get started as you simply have to detail your updates. For example, every time we hit a big milestone I would write an article about it and also share a post on LinkedIn.

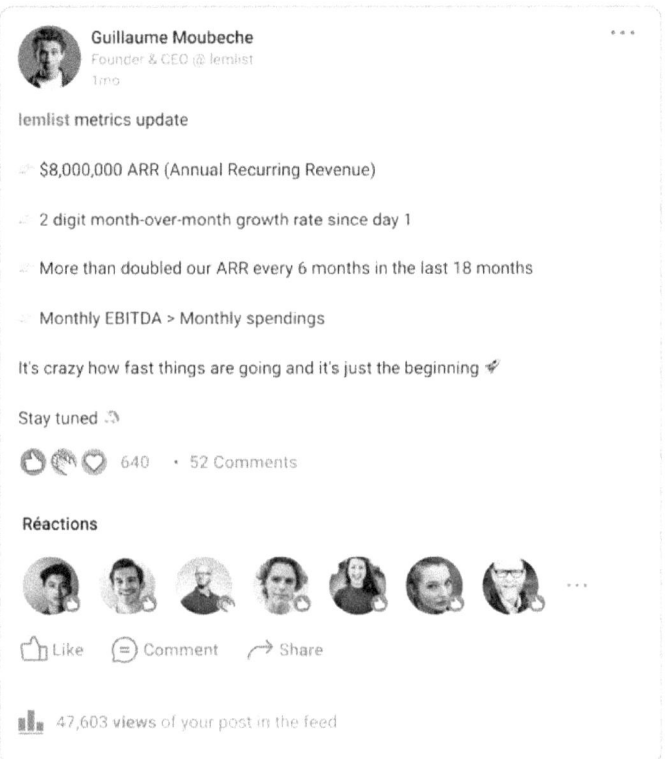

Sharing your wins is a great way to show your audience that you are growing and it's exciting for them to be part of this adventure! It makes them want to follow you, even more, to learn how you managed to do it.

But the "build in public" way of doing things is different from "brag in public". You should also talk about your failures to show the reality in full transparency.

Here for example I recorded a video about how we lost our biggest customer. In the video, I give the exact details of why we lost that customer, how much they were paying, etc. Was I happy about this? Hell no! Was it an easy video to record? Nope…but I explained why it happened. Why, sometimes, your biggest customers are not a fit anymore.

In this case, our biggest customer was a US political party that was using lemlist for the US election. Once the election was finished they obviously didn't have the same needs. So they decided to stop their subscription. Sh*t will always hit the fan in business and it's ok to talk about it because you're not alone.

It will show that you're real, and people will connect with you on a much more emotional level.

In September 2021, I was expecting to make at least $200,000 during a webinar. I documented everything because I was convinced that we would nail the objective. But in the end, it was a massive fail.

We chose the worst date possible, had sound issues during the first 15 minutes of the webinar, I lost my temper because of the technical issue (since I'm part Italian, that can happen sometimes ahah) and the attendance rate was the lowest we had ever experienced due to the date.

I could have just not talked about it and moved on, hidden it under the carpet. But I felt so bad about it and I was so disappointed in myself that I learned a lot! And if by sharing this story I could help other entrepreneurs to feel less lonely or even to learn from my mistakes - then it's all worth it!

Yeah, I won't be that guy who succeeds in everything he does and shares it on social media. But I would be "G.", a guy who's ready to fail as many times as he needs to in order to succeed. A guy that will share all the ups and downs so more people can learn from it, feel less lonely, or even get inspired.

Because to me, transparency is about the good and the bad. And that's why I wrote a post on LinkedIn after that massive fail.

It hurts to write it. But, from an early age, I understood that what hurts me makes me either stronger or smarter. It's obviously 100x more pleasant to talk about how much money we're making and how fast our company is growing.

But talking about failures will help you to achieve 3 things:

1. You'll spend time thinking about why you failed and will learn a LOT.
2. Since failing and talking about it really hurts, you will never make the same mistake twice. Once bitten, twice shy.
3. You'll move on faster because people will show compassion.

When I wrote this LinkedIn post, I was scared. It's always tough for me to put my ego aside and admit that I failed. That sh*t hit the fan, and that I was in that room.

But I realized that the connections you can build during the toughest times are usually the strongest.

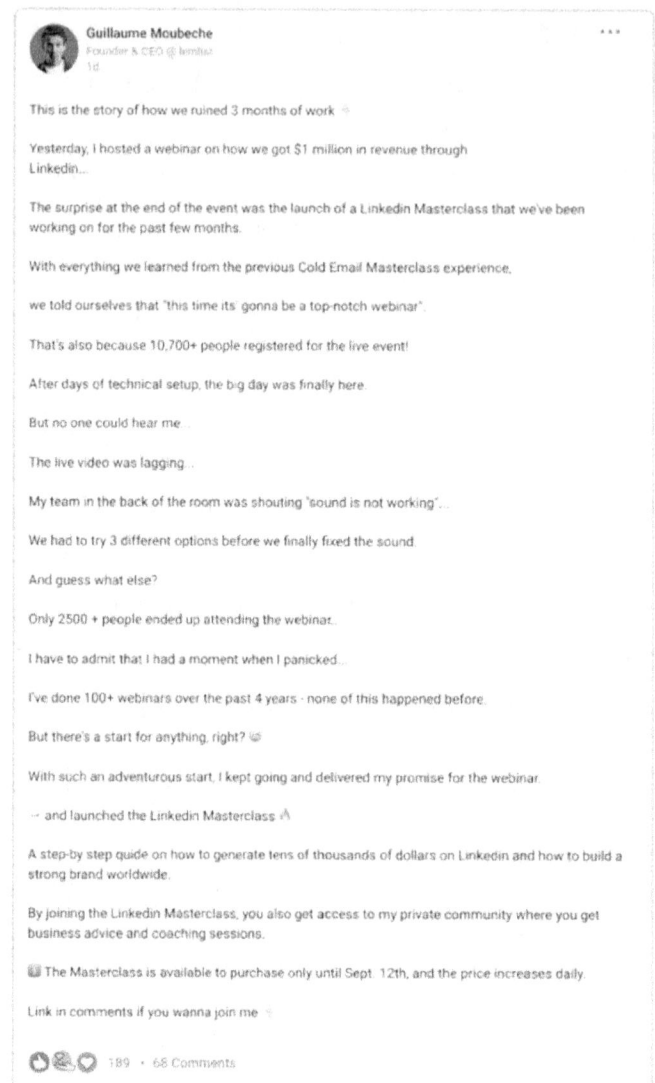

It hurts to write it. But, from an early age, I understood that what hurts me makes me either stronger or smarter. It's obviously 100x more pleasant to talk about how much money we're making and how fast our company is growing. But talking about failures will help you to achieve 3 things:

1. You'll spend time thinking about why you failed and will learn a LOT.

2. Since failing and talking about it really hurts, you will never make the same mistake twice. Once bitten, twice shy.

3. You'll move on faster because people will show

compassion.

When I wrote this LinkedIn post, I was scared. It's always tough for me to put my ego aside and admit that I failed. That sh*t hit the fan, and that I was in that room.

But I realized that the connections you can build during the toughest times are usually the strongest.

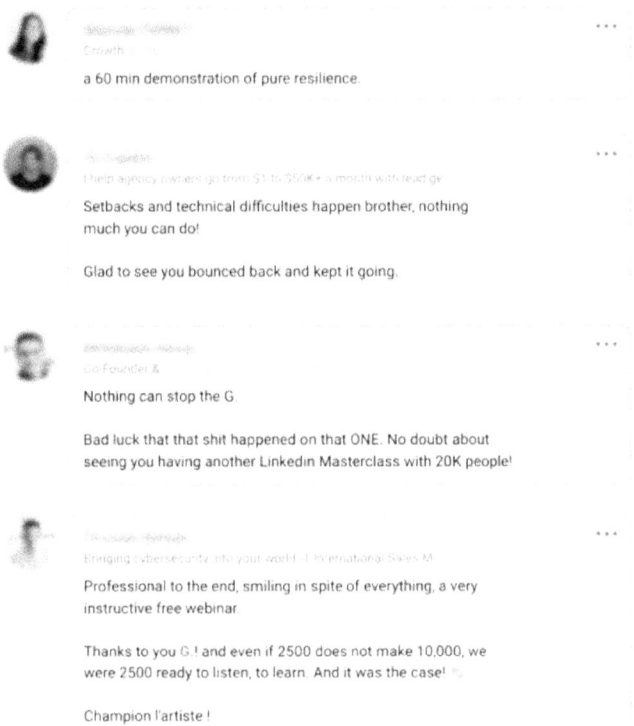

Getting all these comments from lemlisters showed me how important it is to surround yourself with a community of positive people. Tough times will always happen, but who you're going through these times is what matters the most in the end!

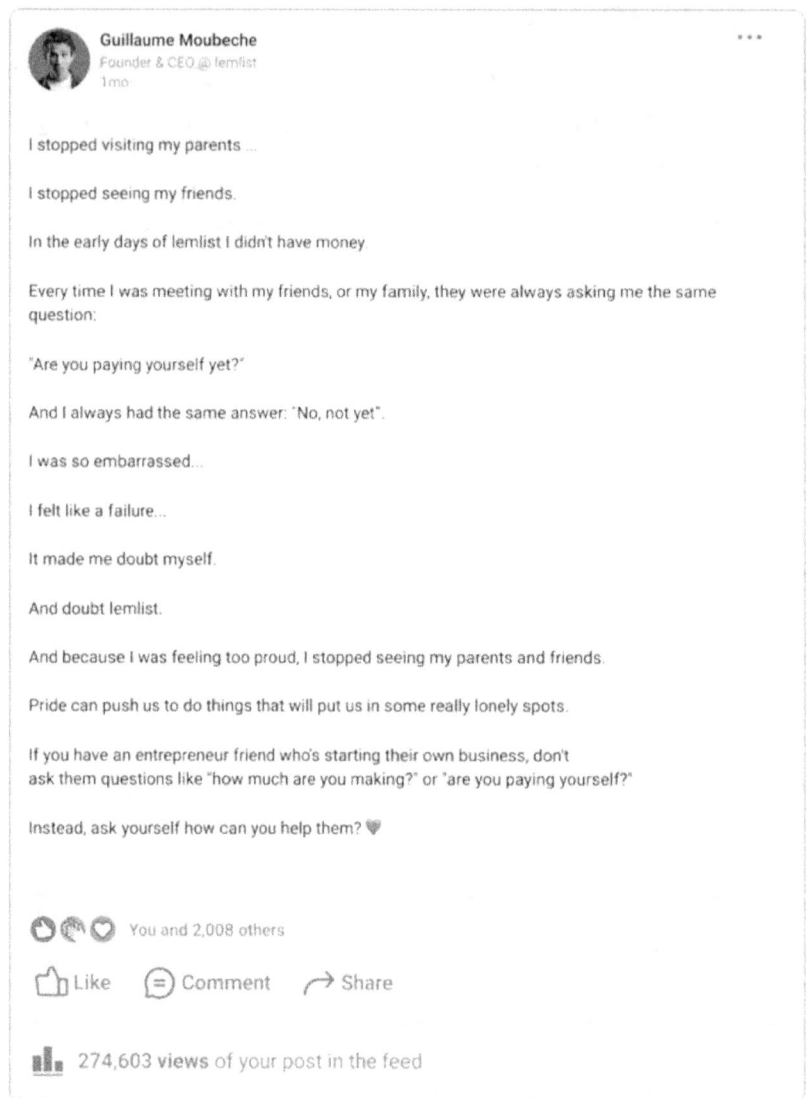

As I said, I've always kept true to myself and there's a reason why. Building a business is a marathon. If you're here for the long run you should focus on two things.

The first one is to be passionate about what you do. The second one is to be yourself.

You can't pretend to be someone else for years. Well…you might, but it's exhausting and so unpleasant to live in a fake world.

3. Be yourself

Social media puts filters on our lives. Everything seems amazing, crazy, adventurous, etc. And that's why people only share the good moments.

But to really build a long-term profitable business you need **to be yourself.** Share everything with no filter. Even if it's painful.

For a long time, I thought that vulnerability was a synonym of weakness. Playing competitive sports for 10+ years, we were never taught to share our feelings openly. Unless it was to showcase how "powerful" or "tough" you could be.

Now I think that it's the opposite. Being vulnerable takes courage. Talking freely about something that you regret, a mistake you've made, or a tough time you went through and that you'd rather never talk about is what will help you connect emotionally with people.

This post tells a story I kept to myself for years. In the early days of lemlist, it was really tough and I knew that some people were going through similar situations.

By being yourself and by allowing yourself not to be perfect, you will show the real you and the relationships you build will be much stronger down the line.

In order to know whether or not you're producing good content, ask yourself whether or not you would be reading the post you're writing and if the "you" from a few months back would enjoy the content. If the answer is "yes" then keep going!

Key learnings

- Never think that you always know better than your customers.
- Being an entrepreneur is about freedom.
- To master something, teach it.
- When growing a business, the success of your users should be your only focus.
- Constraints force creativity.
- When people are eager to learn, there's nothing that can hold them back to reach their full potential.
- What most businesses and founders lack is not the amount of data they have, or what they can measure. They lack guts!
- If your only focus is to make your users/customers successful, there's a 0% chance that you won't succeed over time.
- Building a community helps you get instant feedback about what you're doing.
- When writing content your goal should be for people to share it.
- A great way of positioning yourself as a thought leader is by answering people's questions.
- If you want more money, simply ask for more. The more value you provide, the higher your price should be.
- Being user-centric means getting to know your users better than yourself.
- If you want to be part of the 1% you need to be ready to do the things that 99% of people won't do - period.
- The more engaged your audience is, the easier it will be for you to launch any business successfully.

- Building a business is a marathon. If you're here for the long run you should focus on two things. The first one is to be passionate about what you do. The second one is to be yourself.

S. ALE

Growing a business to $1,000,000 in ARR is already a unique milestone that the vast majority of SaaS businesses will never reach. If you've already reached that milestone, congrats! The next step is going from $1,000,000 to $10,000,000 in ARR.

This 10x growth is also another important milestone for your business and we will discuss later in the last chapter why when you reach $10,000,000 in ARR the valuation of your business can skyrocket. But doing 10x the ARR at that stage is often impossible for companies. Why?

Because you can reach $1M in ARR with a lot of work and grind but that won't be enough to get to $10M. You'll need to build repeatable processes with scalable acquisition channels. In this chapter, we will see how to do so.

Scaling your audience building

For those of you who've been following me on LinkedIn, you know that I post content almost every day.

What I love about LinkedIn is that it's a great place to share valuable tips with a different audience than our customers.

In 2019 my posts got more than 1 million views and I had more than 20,000 people following me on LinkedIn. But then I got banned for life, so I lost everything that I built for 2 years. I tried getting it back for a couple of months, but it didn't work. So I had to start from scratch with a new profile, applying the same strategy that brought me millions of views with my old account.

Since our team has been growing like crazy, we decided to scale it on a higher level, so everyone from the team would be posting at least 3 times per week. For example, Nadja and Simon from the sales team would post actionable sales tips when it comes to doing sales prospecting.

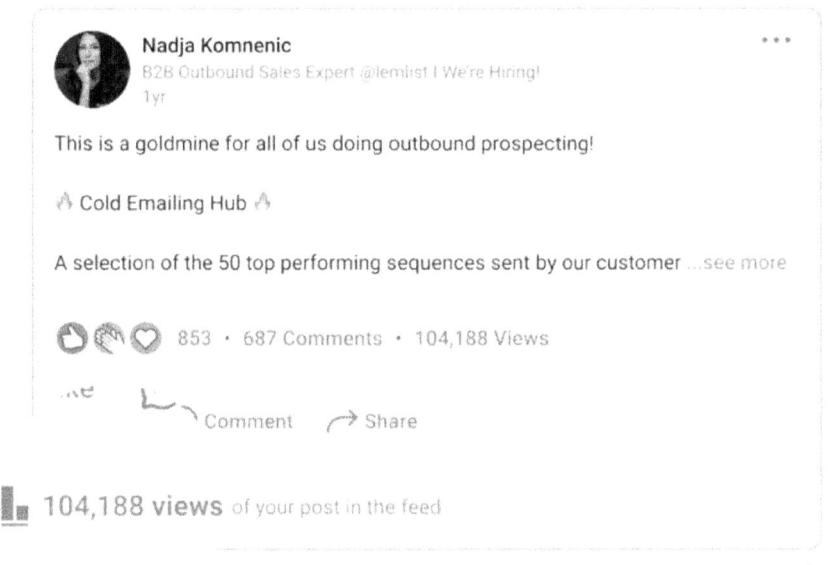

Example of one of Nadja's post

This post worked really well for at least 3 reasons:

1. It starts with a catchy intro that makes people want to read what's next
2. It's relevant and valuable for Nadja's audience
3. It mentions numbers and results that boost credibility

Thanks to valuable posts like this, Nadja was able to build meaningful relationships and close more deals.

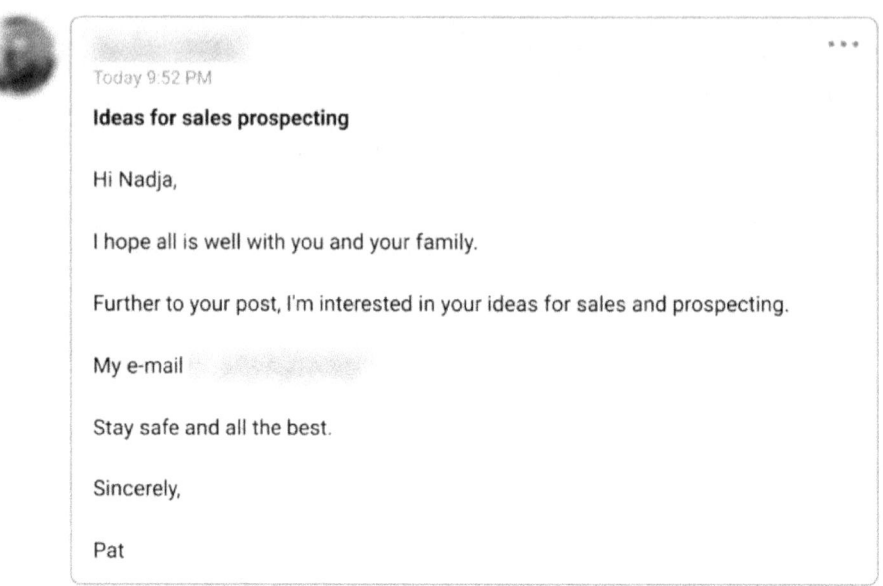

Example of a message received by Nadja after one of her posts

Vuk and Ilya would post about growth guides and acquisition strategies.

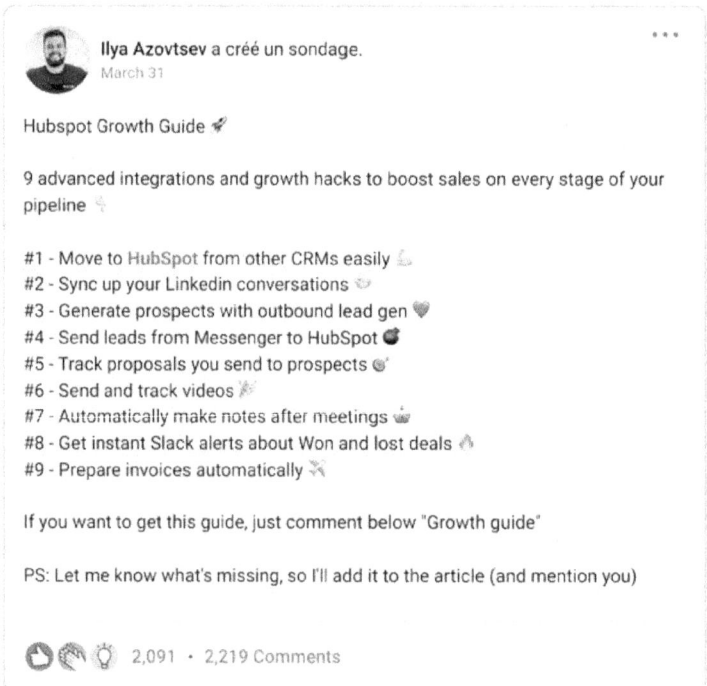

More than 2,000 comments under his post resulted in huge engagement.

Here's why it works:

1. The structure of the post is clear and it generates curiosity since most of the bullet points are unique

"growth hacks"
2. Asking people to comment on your post in order to get additional content is THE best way to get a huge reach. The more people comment, the more your post will be shown to a larger audience.
3. Asking people to get in touch if they have a really cool hack in order to get a mention is a great way to build credibility and show that this growth guide will be updated with all the best hacks.

On my end, I would post about startup tips, user acquisition, and sales. I used to post mainly videos on LinkedIn because, in my opinion, it's a great way to connect with your audience on a much more personal level.

By splitting the different topics between our team members, we were actually able to reach more than 100k people every single week while providing a lot of value.

On top of that, we were able to promote our cold email resources and webinars as well, leading to more exposure for our partners and hence, better relationships.

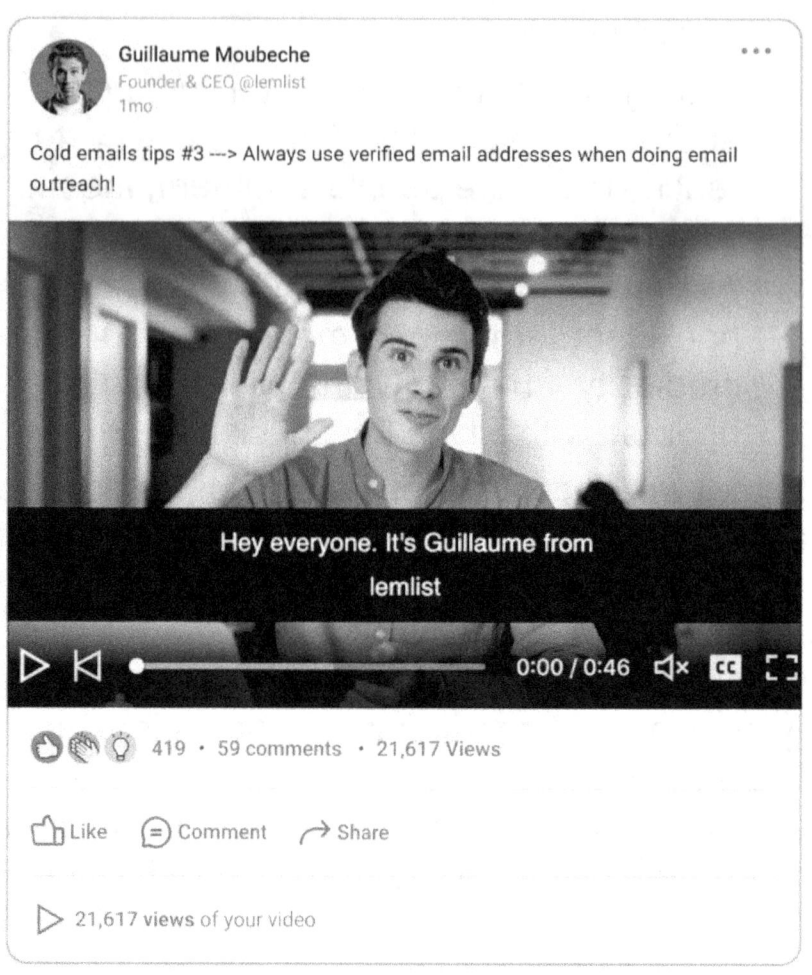

Creating videos on LinkedIn

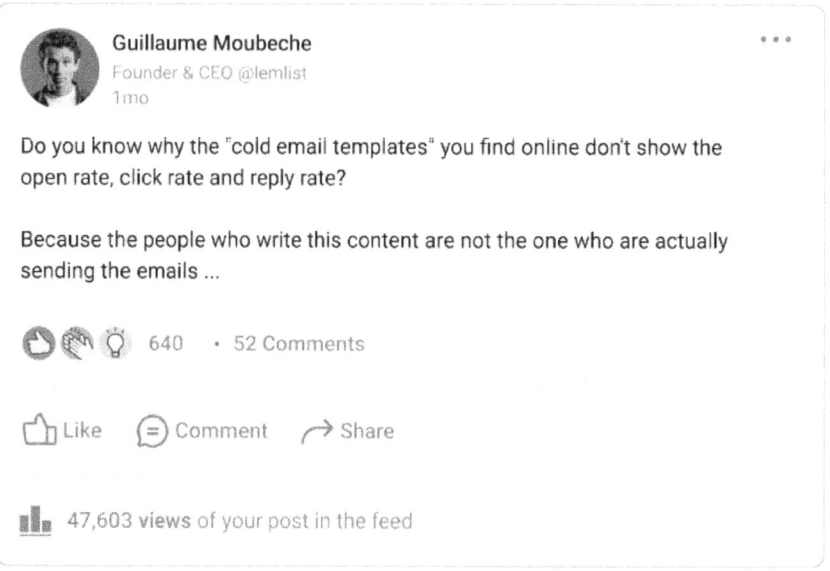

Promoting our Cold Email Hub

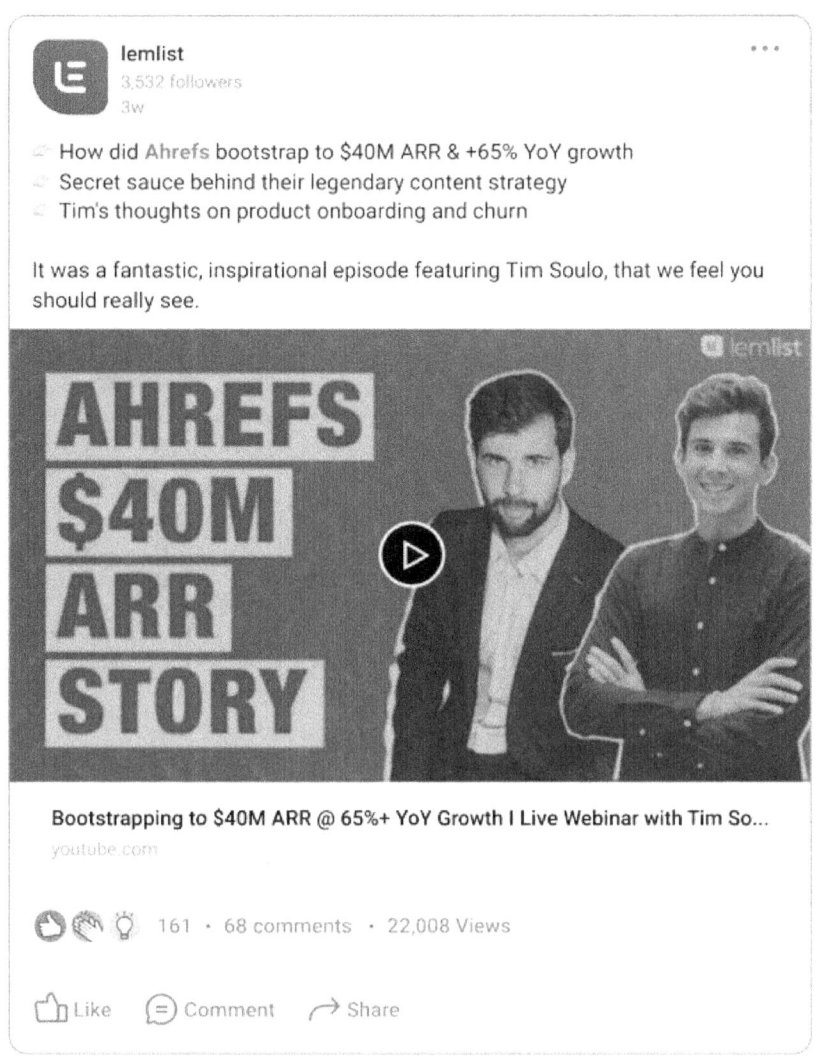

Promoting our Webinars

Even though scaling the way you distribute your content with your team is something that works well, you should leverage the fact that you have a strong audience to partner with others.

Together we're stronger

I love co-marketing[24]! I love it because it is a clear win-win situation! You share your audience with someone else's audience and you grow together!

That's actually why we decided to start a series of interviews with top sales experts in our community!

We had guests such as Aaron Ross, Morgan Ingram, Jill Rowley, and many more! During these live interviews, we talked a lot about sales-related topics, trying to always bring as many actionable tips and pieces of advice as possible!

Interviews, podcasts, and webinars are in my opinion the most underrated way to grow your company. Why? 2 reasons:

1. The power of association

First, let's imagine that you see Barack Obama at a restaurant having lunch with someone. What's your first thought about that person? Probably that this must be someone important! That's the power of association.

When we see two people hanging out together our brain will automatically put them in the same "box". You can leverage this psychological bias to boost your brand and get more people to trust you. How so? By doing interviews with top industry leaders.

By spending time with them asking questions, you get associated with their image and people will tend to perceive you as an expert as well.

2. The power of status

Some people are motivated by fame. Once you get perceived as a thought leader, the chances are high that "status" is something important to you (and there's nothing wrong with that).

By asking people to jump on a podcast or interview with you, you confirm their status. On top of it, people are 100x more likely to accept an interview offer than a networking call. Why?

Status again. Being interviewed shows that you are an expert and it validates your position as a thought leader.

So how exactly do you make sure to be able to interview anyone on earth? Here's the exact template Vuk and I came up with.

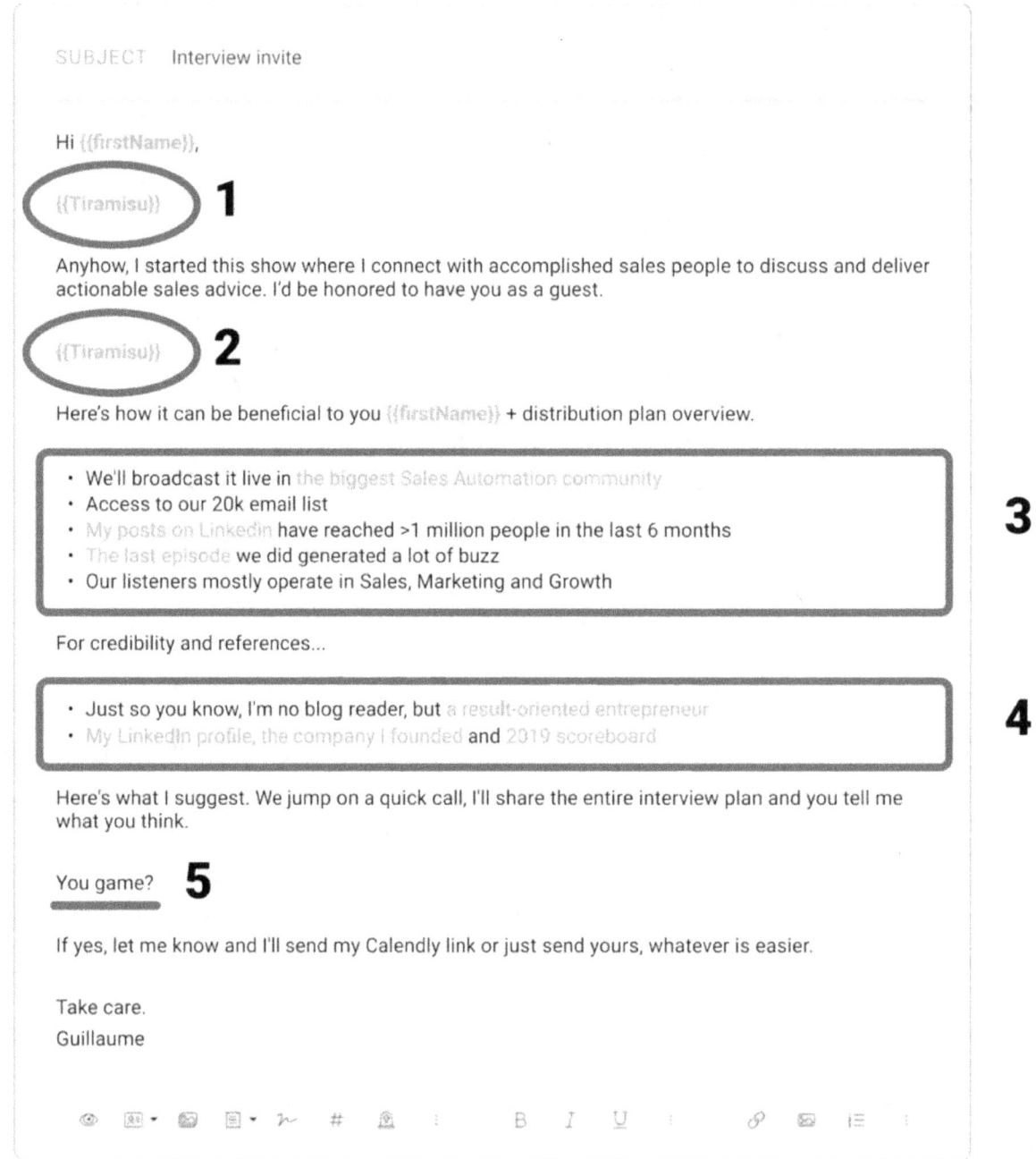

The template we used to reach out to top sales leaders

Here's why it worked:

{{Tiramisu}} tag is replaced with a genuine compliment for that person. In most cases, it consisted of 1–3 sentences where Vuk commented on their recent work and added another sentence on why we admire that person.

"I just finished your episode with Antoine Goret and I really enjoyed the part where he talks about marketing strategies behind Crisp's growth."

{{Tiramisu2}} was changed with our topic proposal. In other words, the topic was discussed with them during the webinar.

"I think it would be great to make this episode about lead scoring and navigating people down the funnel accordingly."

The goal was to show them how their participation will bring them exposure in front of our entire audience and how that's relevant for their brand too.

Credibility is key! We want everybody to know that we are practitioners of our craft with a real track record. Always make it easy for them to answer and know what the next step is.

We had a 70% booking rate from this campaign, which is simply HUUUUGE!

Once our guests were booked we decided to make their life super simple by sending them a very detailed email about 5–7 days prior to the event with everything they should know.

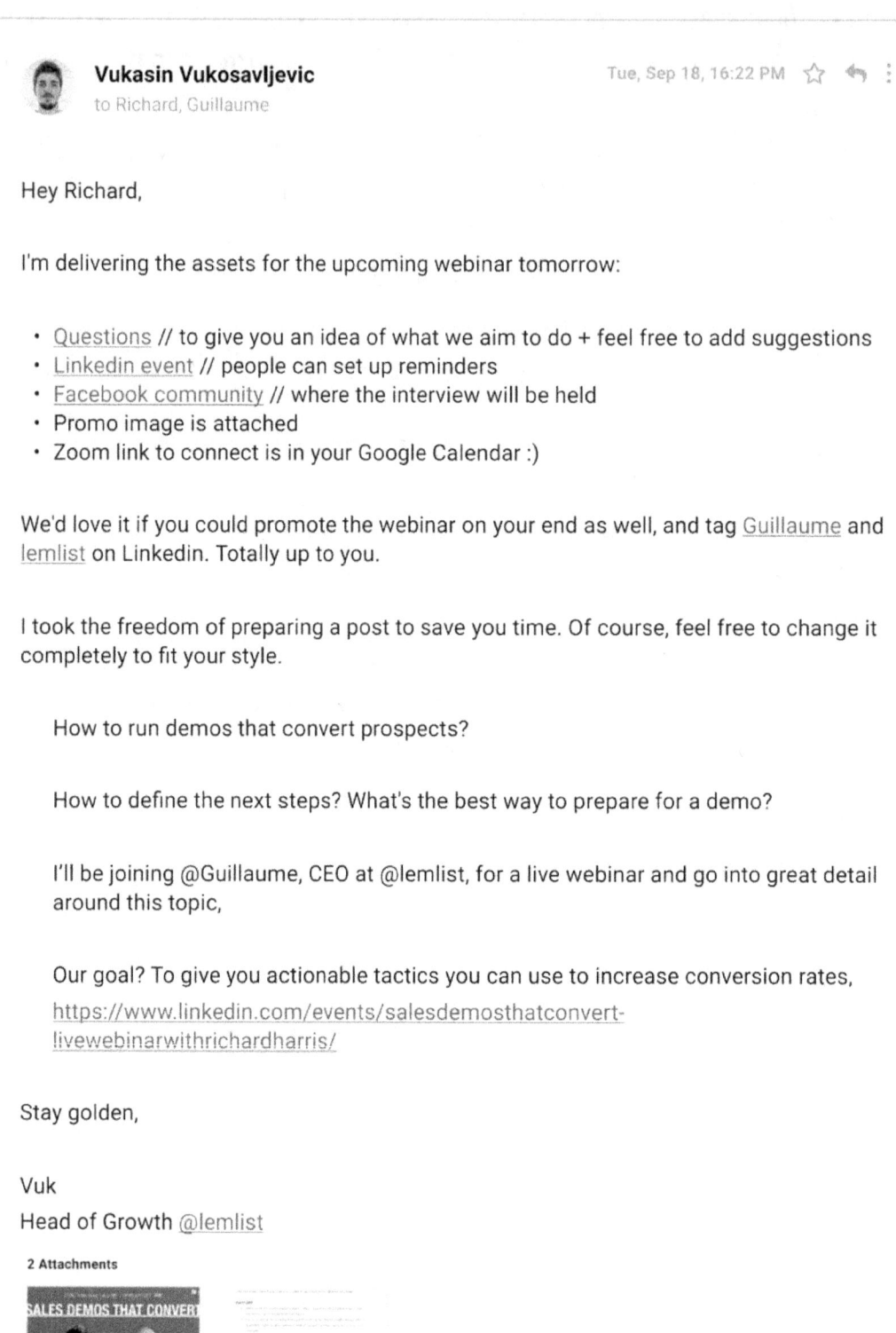

The email we send to each interviewee

prior to the Facebook live

As you can see this email is very well structured and contains:

1. The questions that will be asked with a possibility to edit them or add comments
2. The link to the official event
3. Promo image that can be used for their social posts
4. A ready-to-use copy of a post that they could share with their network

A lot of the experts I interviewed decided to share the link to the event with their audience, which ultimately leads to more people watching the live event.

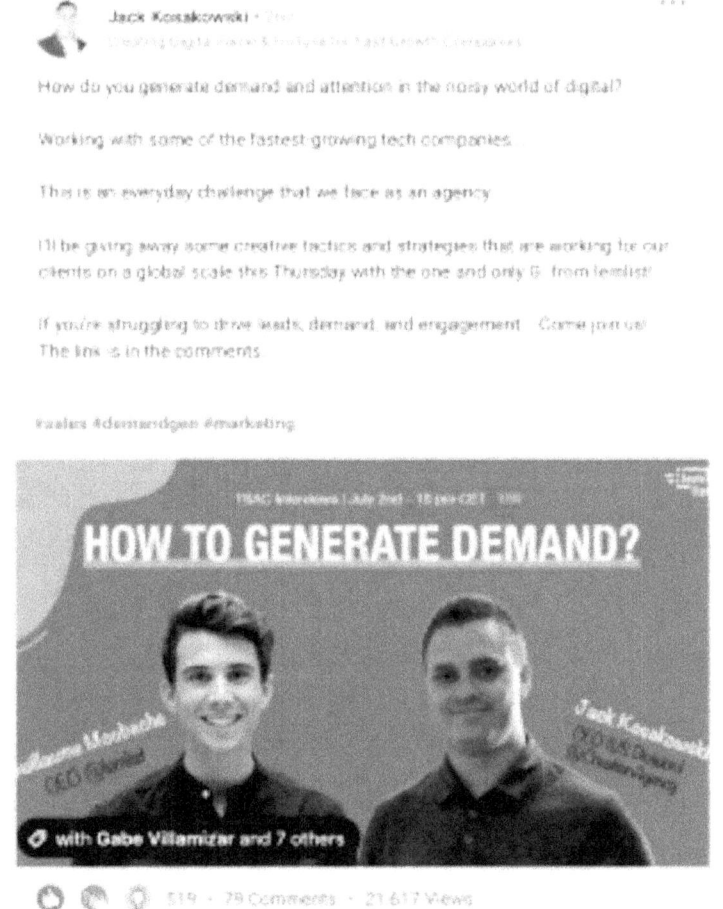

The type of posts our interviewees share on their social network

Each webinar had 100s of participants and the value brought by each expert was so huge that we even decided to open a dedicated section on our website so people could rewatch the live events on YouTube.

On top of that, the more you interview people, the easier it is for you to find new guests. Why? Because the people who you will reach out to will see other influencers being interviewed, which will add social proof and credibility to your podcast or interview series.

I call it the "ladder approach". If you want to get people from the top of the ladder you need to start small and then keep leveling up.

Once the content is recorded you can repurpose it on many different channels as we did here with all the replays of our webinars on the lemlist website.

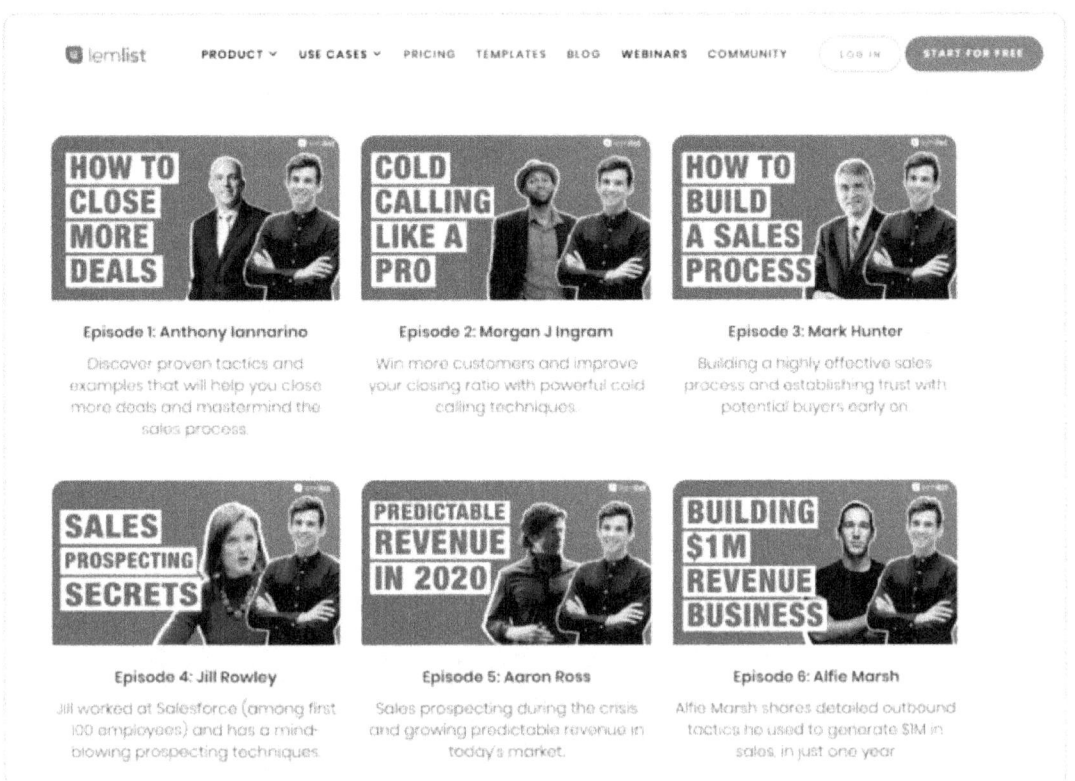

But that's not all. Being seen with industry experts and writing a lot on LinkedIn helped me get much more exposure. I ended up getting invited to speak at a lot of international events, including SaaStock with some top names from the marketing industry.

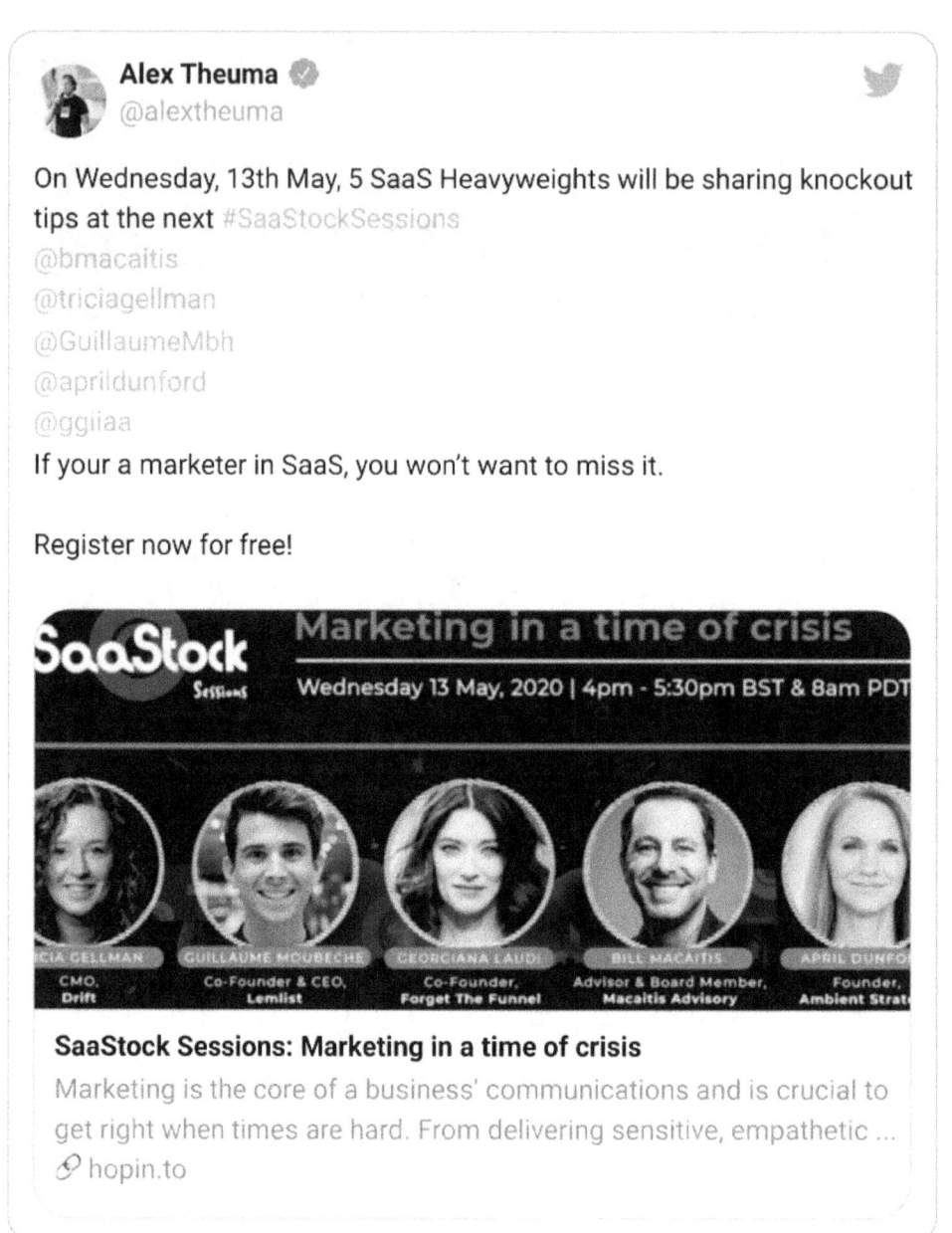

Being invited as a speaker into top events like SaaStock

All the interviews I did were actually extremely helpful for me to learn new things from top sales experts and build really strong relationships.

Aaron Ross even invited me to speak during his summit on how to build a B2B outbound sales strategy from scratch!

Another really cool event organized by Aaron's Ross team

If you don't know Aaron Ross he's the guy who helped Salesforce grow from $0 to $100M in revenue. He wrote the bible of sales 20 years ago and has been recognized as an outbound expert.

All of these online events were a great way to bring as much value as possible to a new audience, which then drove a lot of new revenue and opportunities for us!

Build a family, not a community

With more than 18,000 members, lemlist family has become our unfair advantage over the years, and that's because we decided to build a family and not a community.

> Communities die, families prosper.
>
> – Guillaume Moubeche

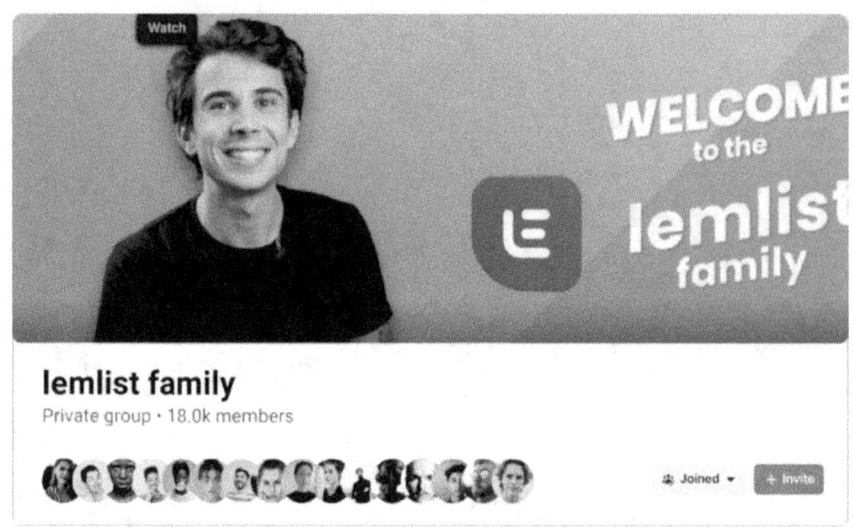

*lemlist family - the biggest community around
Sales, Automation, and Growth*

What I've seen when people build a community around their product or service is that they either let their users run the community by themselves OR they try to get instant ROI on every single action they do…

In the first case, most often it turns into a complete mess when it becomes too big as posts are not organized, and some people will seek help without a response…

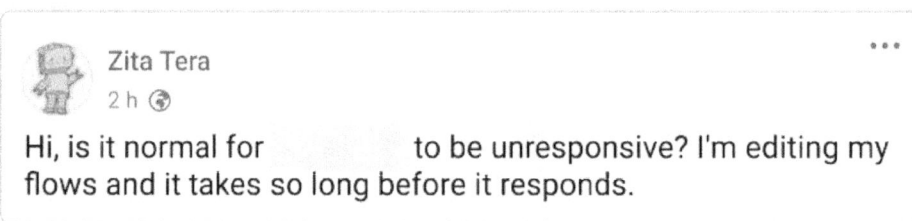

*A person seeking for help with no response
in a group with 90,000 people…*

The second case often leads to a dead community after a while since people don't like to be sold all the time.

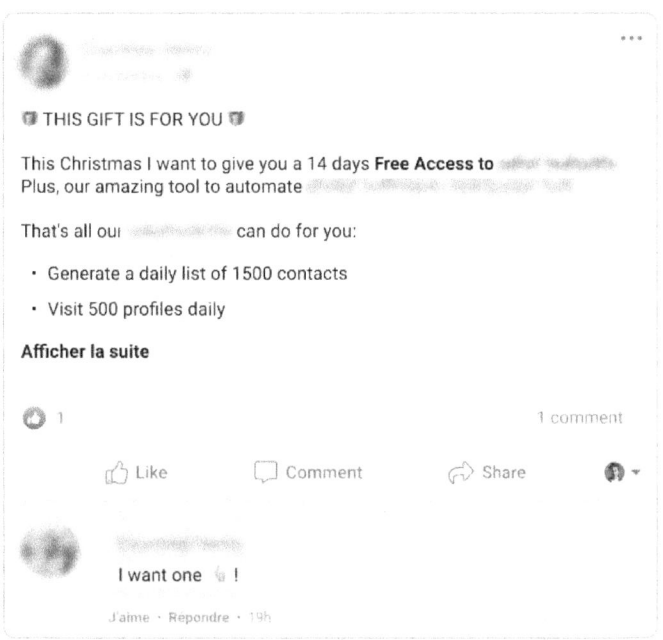

*Example of a sales post made by an admin
with 0 engagement except himself*

In our case, we've decided that the lemlist *family* will be a safe place for people to seek help, get the best insights about sales automation, get inspired, and get better at sales prospecting.

Post in the lemlist family -

35 comments from people willing to help out

Obviously, we also share product updates and big announcements, but we do it in a way where we know that our users are always involved in the growth process.

Making an announcement in the community

Having such a cool family has allowed us to build trust and grow with our customers. We don't pretend to know everything, but we strive to listen to our users and find the best solutions to their problems...

No product, no money

We see more and more companies that are Product-led growth, which means that their growth is essentially driven by their product. We can think of companies like Figma, Airtable, or more recently Notion.

Investing heavily in your product can make a major difference in your growth, and that's what we did at lemlist.

Hiten Shah said that when your team grows, we too often see the quality of the product decreasing…

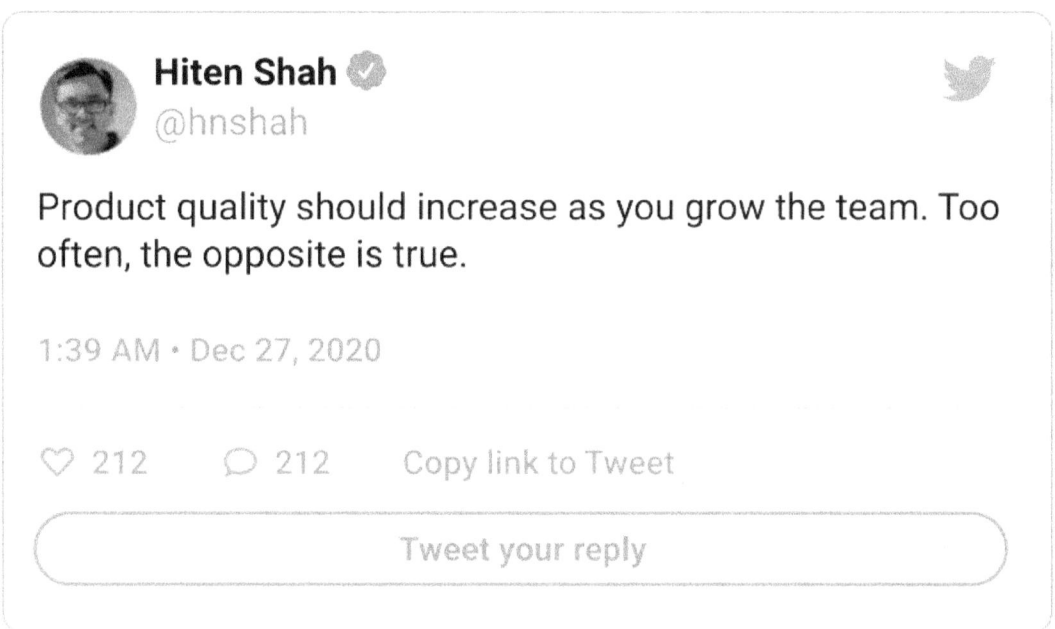

In my opinion, this can happen for the following reasons:
1. The founding team focused on adding new features as quickly as possible without thinking too much about the scaling phase (poor documentation, technical debt, infrastructure not made to scale).
2. The recruitment process is broken, and the onboarding of junior developers only leads to more bugs and more issues.
3. The company has decided to go up-market and has started building more and more custom features making the product less and less user friendly.

That's why it was the right decision to start lemlist with my two co-founders, two technical guys with 25+ years of experience each.

Since one of my co-founders previously managed a team of 50+ developers, he knew that experience beat numbers.

At lemlist, our tech team is composed of engineers with an average of 15+ years of experience.

We never focused on the number of engineers in our team, we only focused on the talent of the people we hired.

Team is everything

This might sound obvious, but your team will be the most important success factor of your company as you grow.

The biggest challenge we had growing so quickly was to scale the team accordingly. I've made a lot of mistakes when it comes to hiring and managing the team and here are a few things I wish I knew when I started:

A. Never make compromises with your core values

At first, I didn't really understand why core values were crucial to a company. Over time, I realized that your core values are the best ways to determine whether you should hire someone or not.

lempire's core values

For example, continuous growth and curiosity are key at lemlist. So during the interview process, my goal is to understand to what extent people are curious enough to learn new things by themselves.

Hence typical questions could be:

- What have you learned recently?
- Do you listen to any podcasts? Which ones?
- What books have you read recently?
- What have you learned from the last article/book that you've read?
- Have you completed any courses recently? What was it about? Can you highlight your key learnings?

When it comes to making important decisions, having clear values will make the decision process much smoother because you'll always be able to tell whether or not it is part of your values. Which leads to my second lesson.

B. Hire fast - fire fast

Hiring is an art...the more you practice, the better you get at it. BUT hiring someone is not an exact science. That's why our recruiting process is really fast - from 48 hours to a few days before getting a final answer.

If it's not a good fit, we will always give detailed feedback in order for the person to understand why we think that this position is not a match.

Interviews are a great way to filter candidates but you'll only know if someone is a good fit after working with him/her for at least a few weeks.

Sometimes, you will realize that someone who was incredibly talented during the interview process is simply not a good fit for the company...and that's a very unpleasant feeling because it shows you that you were wrong…But in my experience, the faster you let that person go, the better.

Keeping someone who is not a good fit will only make your team less efficient and less motivated. This brings us to one of the most important points...

C. Talent brings talent

The key source of talented people is actually the people you've already hired.

At lemlist, 75% of the people we've hired came from a recommendation from someone already in the team.

ena 9:35 PM
I worked with both, that is why I recommended them - I do not recommend people I do not know will work
Ariana was in my team and I trained her, worked in English - perfect

*Ena recommended Ariana, who joined the lemlist family
a week after I received that message*

Make sure that your employees are happy and involve the whole team in the hiring process.

D. Hiring is like selling

At first, I thought that hiring people was gonna be easy. Candidates were rushing to our job offers and craving to work for lemlist...

The truth is that if you want to get the best people to join you, you need to learn how to sell your company. Hence, understanding what the person is looking for and finding whether or not they are a good fit is essential.

Guillaume Moubeche <guillaume@lemlist.com>
to Nadja

Hey Nadja,

Vuk told me you had a call with him, so I'd like to give you additional context:

Our goal at lemlist in the next 3 years is to totally change the face of sales automation.

We want to make it more human, more personalized and funnier! If you've been working in sales and especially in business development you know that sales prospecting is NOT fun! However, we truly believe that it should be fun! And we know that's something we can change as we really want to help people connect with each other in the right way!

The role I pictured for you is matching this ambition.

I want you to represent that change and I think that you have the charisma to do it.

I feel like women are not well enough represented in the sales world while most of the time they are outperforming their male colleagues.

You will learn tons of things and we will work all as a team to really kick asses worldwide.

My goal is for you to be seen as a top sales leader and we will help you accomplish that by boosting your personal branding on LinkedIn. We will also work together to build the future of sales processes including some huge changes in lemlist (we are going multichannel very soon).

I understand that you have a new project going on, but this is a once in a lifetime opportunity.

I'd be happy to hop on a call again to answer all your questions and discuss that further, but I'd like to get an answer by the end of the week.

Talk to you soon!

Cheers,
G.

The email I sent to Nadja (our current head of business development) to convince her to join us.

When finding perfect candidates, make sure that your vision is aligned with where they see themselves in a few years.

Building a startup is an exciting adventure, and if you find ambitious people, they need to trust you and understand that you will help them achieve their goals.

E. Build a hiring process fast

I mentioned that hiring was not an exact science, but it's still an art. And the more structure you have when hiring people, the more predictable and repeatable it becomes, and thus, *whoever is in charge of the interview*.

Make sure that all candidates undergo the same hiring process, so you're sure not to miss any flaws and hence reduce your risks.

F. There is no silver bullet in management

I grew up playing a competitive team sport, and to me, great coaching was a synonym for tough coaching. And I guess that my management style was in some ways similar to that…tough but fair…

However, I realized that this management style had a negative impact on some people and that I needed to adapt. My biggest learning was that communication and trust is the key to the success of a company.

If you don't communicate and if there's no trust, your team won't be able to give you feedback about your management style.

People shouldn't be "scared" to tell the CEO that he fucked up or that his management style is OFF. Everyone makes mistakes, so it's important to make sure everyone knows they can tell it to you directly.

G. Don't be a perfectionist

As a founder, it was extremely difficult for me to delegate at first.

I was the only person managing sales, marketing, and growth at lemlist for a long time, and having others do what I considered as "my job" was tough because it was never exactly the way I wanted it…

But as time went by, I understood that it will never be exactly as I want it to be, because it's not me doing it.

I loved the way Julian Shapiro talked about the 70/10/80

Principle of delegation:

> "Find someone who can do what you do at 70% the success rate. Teach them the extra 10% and be okay with 80%."
>
> – Julian Shapiro

Building on that, if you want to help people get better at what they do, you have to build processes from day 1.

> The enemy of delegation is perfectionism ...
>
> – Guillaume Moubeche

Process rhymes with success

Do you think it's a coincidence? Hell no! Or maybe, there are tons of words that end up like this. Like "princess". But using that word would not make sense here.

If you've been reading my articles you know that I love processes. Processes are reliable, predictable, and the easiest way to understand what went wrong if sh*t hits the fan…whether it's for onboarding new employees, sharing knowledge, or even structure, the way you work, our processes have been a real game-changer.

At lemlist, we structure everything in Notion. Each department has its own processes, and everything is accessible to everyone. Below is how our sales resources are organized.

Goals
- Goals
- KPIs
- Pipeline

Daily
- Agendas
- Projects

Planning
- Routines
- Ideas

Learning
- Onboarding Playbook
- New hire Onboarding
- Sales Process
- Writing
- Demo calls: Archite...
- Persona / Value Pro...
- Our market
- Research
- Communities
- Thought leaders to f...
- Cold Emailing Hub
- Delivrability Checkl...

Other
- Tools
- Referrals
- Submit Expenses
- lemdesk

Core
- lempire story
- Why lemlist

If you dig deeper, you'll end up with sub documentation for each step of the sales process.

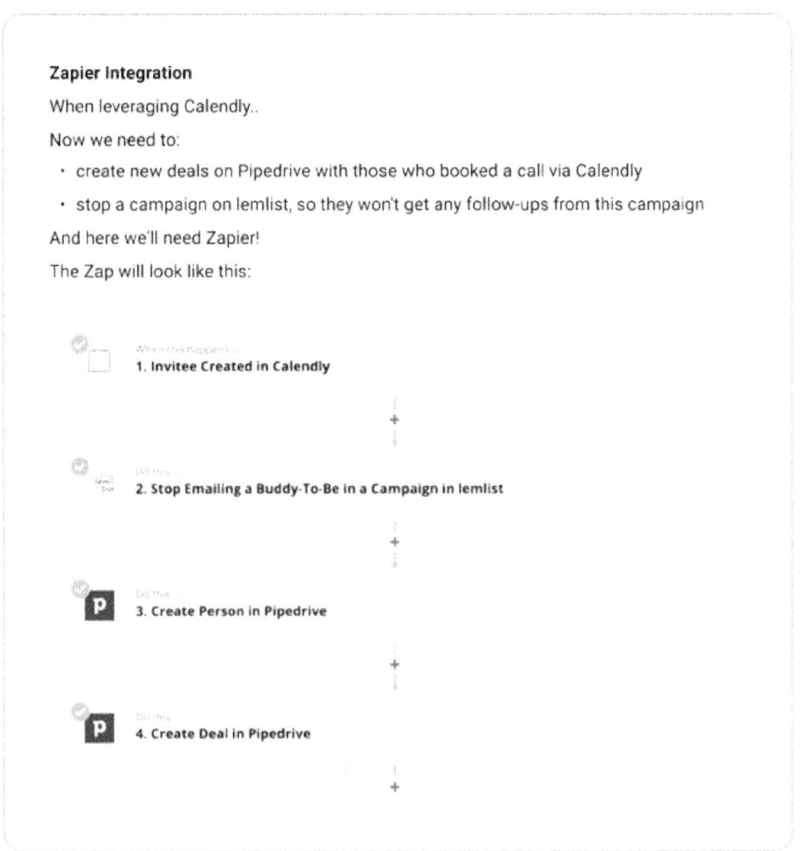

For example, the screenshot below shows the important things to know for setting up our Pipedrive CRM so that when someone is new or has a doubt, he/she can refer directly to that specific page.

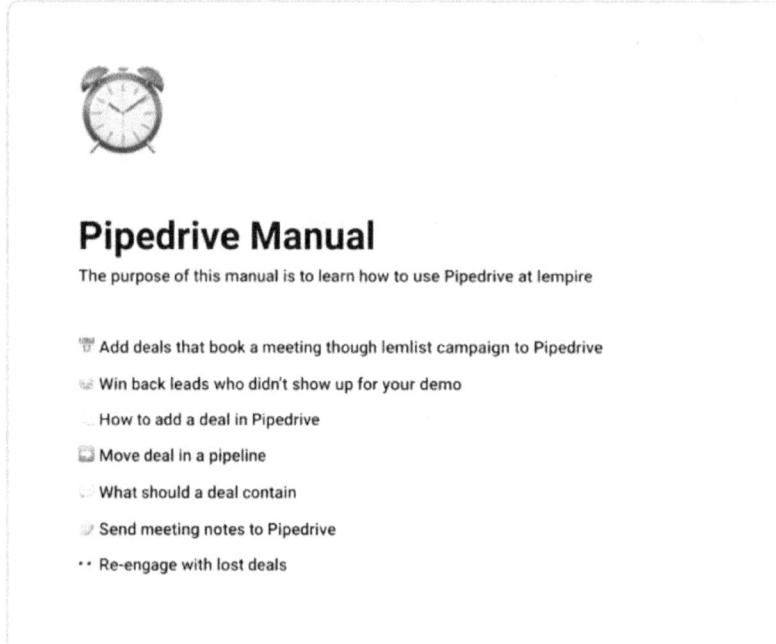

In each subsection, you will find a detailed tutorial with screenshots and a video tutorial that has been tested and approved by the team.

Creating clear processes makes the information easy to understand for everyone in the team which allows us to train and ramp up people in a much faster way.

Be transparent

Unfortunately, that word has been overused, especially in the startup world. Since "transparency" is becoming cool, most companies are putting "transparency" in their core values, but the reality is that they are not transparent at all.

Ask a "transparent" startup what their ARR is, or how much their EBITDA is, or even what the CEO's salary is.

If you don't get these answers, ask them what they mean by transparency...and leave…

Some people will tell you that it's easy to be transparent when you're growing fast and have crossed the $10m ARR mark...true! But if you check our blog, you'll see that I was transparent from day 1, even when our revenue was close to 0.

When growing a company, there are 3 levels of transparency, and each of them taught me something important.

Level 1. Being fully transparent with your team

When building a startup, the people you hire are going to become your brand ambassadors. Whether it's because they are doing sales demos, helping people solve a specific issue, or even just networking. Your team will reflect your company culture. And that's why they need to be 100% involved.

Every person at lempire is passionate about the project and considers lemlist like his/her own baby.

We only hired people who were passionate about our mission to help 1,000,000 entrepreneurs build and grow profitable businesses.

But that's not it. If you want your team to fully trust you, it's important to share all the ups and downs with them.

Being transparent from the start with every single person who joined our team has helped us build such a strong culture and involve people even more.

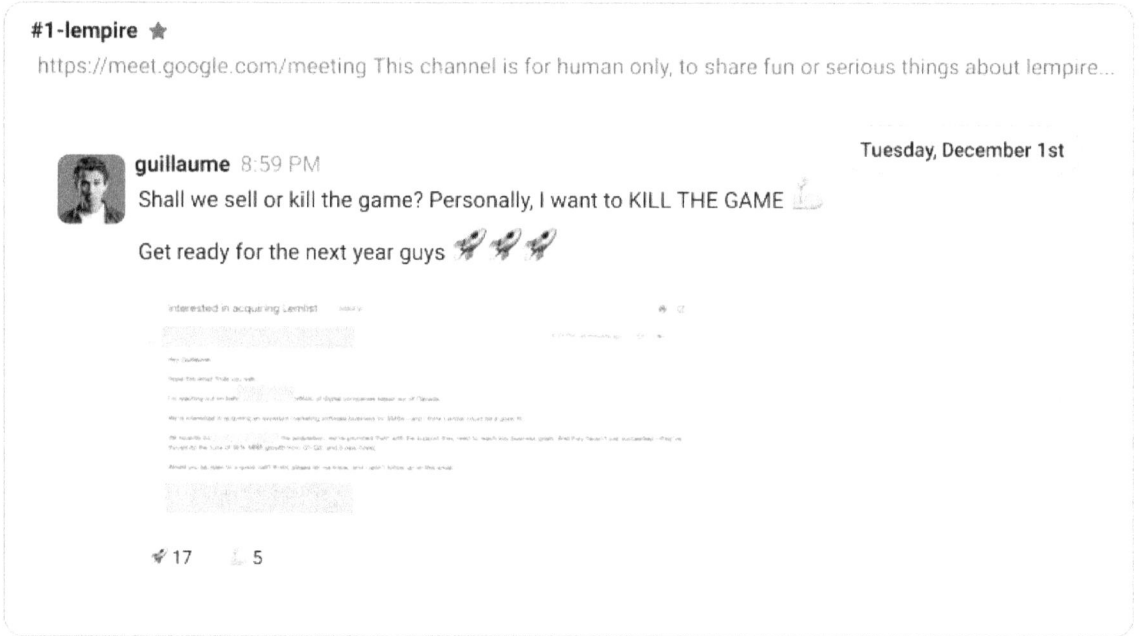

*Sharing an acquisition offer with the team
and reminding the trajectory for 2022*

How do you want people to be involved in the company's growth if they don't know the big picture or the issues and challenges you're facing?

Not telling them when sh*t hits the fan is like expecting everyone around you to be covered in sh*t without letting them know why, and then expecting them to handle the cleaning.

Level 2. Being fully transparent with your customers

When you look at how companies handle communication crises, you'll see that when things go south they either don't say anything or use shady answers…but let me tell you something…

WE ALL MAKE MISTAKES! Me, you, your customers, your team…sh*t happens! That's life!

In the early days of lemlist we had the biggest bug ever on our software. A bug that, when checking the messages people were sending to our support team, made me think that it would cost us 25% of our customer base…

That probably was the scariest time for me…I had to write an email explaining everything to our clients…

Together with my co-founders, we decided to be fully

transparent by giving all the technical details behind it and explaining our plan to prevent it from happening again.

To my surprise, most of the messages received were to support us! The fact that we were vulnerable and transparent just made us look more human.

Level 3. Being fully transparent with the outside world

If you're reading this book and have read my previous articles, you know that I share everything.

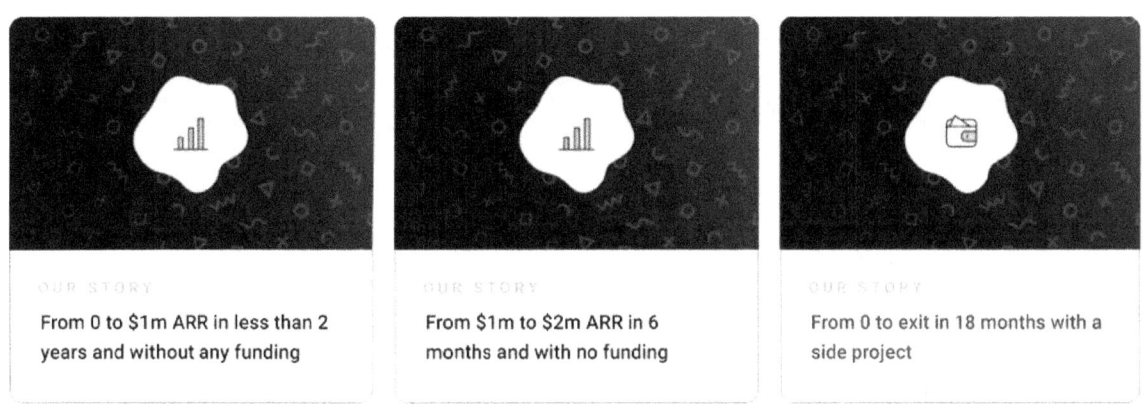

Sharing each step of our journey in detailed articles

I started sharing all our metrics from day 1. The first time I did it live was when Nathan Latka interviewed me on his podcast, "The top entrepreneurs". I think the more you share your metrics (MRR, Churn, LTV, etc.) with the world, the more you feel the need to do better the next time you share something.

Sharing metrics and bonuses during Nathan's interview

Every time I share what we've accomplished, I always try to state our future goals as well. By doing so, I hold myself accountable in public for what we want to achieve. For me, it has been a huge driver of our growth.

The higher you set your goals, the more things you'll put in place to reach them.

On top of it, when I publicly document why we reached a specific milestone, it allows me to reflect on everything we've accomplished.

It allows me not only to go back over all these things that we've done the right way but also to understand what we could have done better. And that part usually gives you tons of ideas for what you can start doing. And gives you a lot of clarity for what needs to be done!

But that's not the only reason why I'm doing this. Remember that story about my friend Max? The day I first read his article about how they acquired their first customers, I got so inspired!

It's crazy how one single article can change your perspective on how you want to do things. When I read the article it felt like I was part of their journey.

That's why I decided to do the same. With my articles, interviews, podcasts, this book. I want everyone who has started their business (or who is thinking of starting one) to see that it's possible to build and grow a business with very little resources.

Show them what we were able to accomplish with only $1000. I want to change people's lives with words. The same way my life changed when I read that article for the first time.

The other reason, that you probably already know by now, is that the more you share honest stuff, the more people will relate to what you say.

The more people relate to your story, the more they trust you and want to follow you on your journey. And when people want to follow your journey, they usually share it with their friends. This will ultimately bring more people to follow your journey, hence your company will get more visibility.

Getting media coverage

When we think about media coverage we tend to think about the big names in the press such as Forbes, New York Times or Tech crunch. However, media coverage is much broader than that.

With more and more bloggers and podcasts, the media scene has dramatically changed in the last few years. You can find bloggers that get more reach than media sites, and podcasters who are getting paid 1000x more than journalists.

Because of this broader distribution network, you have better chances to get coverage as a bootstrapped founder.

If you look at the general press, you'll see that when they mention startups, it's usually to showcase the biggest amount of money raised by startups. The bigger the fundraising round is, the more clicks and traffic the media gets.

So how the hell are you supposed to get media coverage as a bootstrapped startup?

For all media you'll need to have 2 things:
1. A compelling story to tell
2. A story that is in line with the content strategy of the media/podcast/blog where you want to be interviewed.

In the last few years, I've been interviewed on 100+ podcasts, TV shows, journals, and blogs of different sizes. And even though there are some differences, overall the strategy is the same.

But you need to be careful. The size of the publication is really not correlated to the business you will generate from it. It's the same as your audience size.

> It's better to have 1000 hardcore fans rather than 100,000 inactive followers.
>
> – Guillaume Moubeche

Let me tell you a story of two friends of mine that we will call Bob and Mike. They both started on LinkedIn willing to build and grow their agency. Bob was super focused on growing his network as fast as possible, so he added pretty much everyone he could from students to HR leaders and even dentists.

However, Mike decided to only connect with specific entrepreneurs, spending time to personalize the connection request message.

Hey G. I really enjoyed reading your book about how you grew lemlist to a $150M company in 3.5 years. I'd love to follow your journey on Linkedin! **See less**

After a year, Mike had 1000 connections in his network while Bob had 10x that. They would both post regularly on LinkedIn and Bob would get much more reach and traction. However, he will never get any leads from his posts…

Mike on his end, being super targeted and focused on entrepreneurs, would get fewer views and engagement because of his smaller audience. But after every single post, he would get a few messages from his audience saying that they'd like to have a chat with him.

Using this super-targeted approach, Mike started to make thousands of dollars each week while Bob only got likes and reach.

The take is that you should always remember your goal when building an audience. It's really easy to fall into the trap of "vanity metrics". Of course, likes, comments, and the reach of your post will make you feel good about what you did. But that's not the goal.

The goal is to bring as much value as possible to a specific target audience so you can build a business around it.

And that's why you should always choose relevancy overreach when targeting podcasts to be featured on.

1. Getting on any Podcast

At first, I thought that each person running a podcast would actually reach out to the person they wanted to interview. That's true…but not entirely.

Running a podcast or a blog with interviews is demanding and having someone reaching out can make your life easier. So I wanted to share this secret framework we've used to get on any podcast.

It's built around 3 questions:

- What's in it for them?

Try to understand who they are, why they are doing this podcast, and see how you can help them achieve their goals.

- What story do you want to tell?

If you understand their audience you need to find a compelling story for them so they don't feel like you're on the podcast simply to promote your product/service.

- How can you help them get more views?

Every single person doing a podcast or running a blog is trying to get a bigger audience. If you help them understand that you'll help them achieve just that within your outreach - it's a win!

And here is the exact email we used to get featured on 10s of podcasts when we started the scale mode with lemlist. Let's break it down to understand why it worked so well.

SUBJECT I've Got a Story for You **{{firstName}}**

Hi {{firstName}}

My name is Guillaume and I'm the CEO and co-founder of lemlist.

I've listened to a few episodes on your podcast and I think you guys are doing some fantastic work.

{{Sentence}}

I'd love to be your guest on the show.

For the past 1.5 years I've been building lemlist, an email outreach tool based on dynamic personalization (text, images, videos, landing pages). Our tool helps businesses get more replies to cold emails, and makes their sales process far more contextual and human.

After listening to your work, I believe your audience might enjoy hearing about my journey. My promise to you is that I'll share an honest and practical story - signing 10k customers and growing 30% MoM in a vastly competitive market.

Of course, there's a lot of other topics we could be talking about too:

1) How to make personalization and automation work together
2) Building a 2.5X community on Facebook and why that matters so much
3) Leveraging LinkedIn for greater engagement and business growth
4) Bootstrapping your SaaS towards profit by focusing on Product and Brand

For references and credibility, you can check out my LinkedIn profile and an episode I did with Nathan Latka.

Anyways, I'd love to hear your ideas and would be thrilled to join **{{Podcast}}**. If you're up for it, lemme know.

Much love,

Guillaume

Subject line: I've Got a Story for You

Here, the subject line is intriguing - everyone loves good stories! And that's something you should always aim for: trigger curiosity with the subject line. Why? Because if you want people to read your email, they first need to open it. Then comes the email itself. Let's take a look.

Hi {{firstName|team}},

My name is Guillaume and I'm the CEO and Co-Founder of lemlist. I've listened to a few episodes on your podcast and I think you guys are doing some fantastic work.

A little compliment is always nice and is a great way to break the ice. But make sure to make it specific so it doesn't look automated and shows that you actually care.

{{Sentence}}

This personalized sentence for each person you reach out to is key - it shows that you care and that it's not a fully automated email sent to everyone. You can also use this personalization sentence at the very beginning of your email so they know from the start that you are reaching out to them specifically.

I'd love to be your guest on the show. For the past 1.5 years, I've been building lemlist, an email outreach tool based on dynamic personalization (text, images, videos, landing pages). Our tool helps businesses get more replies to cold emails, and makes their sales process far more contextual and human.

About me - this section gives a bit of context, but it could have been removed.

After listening to your work, I believe your audience might enjoy hearing about my journey. My promise to you is that I'll share an honest and practical story - signing 10k customers and growing 30% MoM in a vastly competitive market.

Of course, there are a lot of other topics we could be talking about too:

1. *How to make personalization and automation work together*
2. *Building a 2.5K community on Facebook and why that matters so much*
3. *Leveraging LinkedIn for greater engagement and business growth*
4. *Bootstrapping your SaaS towards profit by focusing on Product and Brand*

That's the part where you sell yourself and help them picture a story

For references and credibility, you can check my LinkedIn profile (link) and an episode I did with Nathan Latka (link).

Showing you're a real person and that you've already done it

Anyways, would love to hear your ideas and would be thrilled to join {{Podcast}}. If you're up for it, lemme know.
Much love,
{{signature}}

2. Getting featured in the press and on TV

To get featured in the press, you need to put yourself in the shoes of the journalists. They tend to write a lot and they sometimes lack inspiration.

In this book, we've seen that every solution you can find to a specific problem can generate business. In this case, the problem is the lack of inspiration or the lack of a good story. The solution is to make their lives easy. Making people's life easy is one of the most underrated skills in business…but that's a topic for another time.

For example, you could pre-write an article for a journalist and then have them revise it.

Here's an example of the outreach we did for journalists that led to being featured in multiple tech publications.

SUBJECT   We turned down $30M from a VC

Hi {{firstName}}.

{{Tiramisu}}

Anyhow, based on your previous work, I'd say you're a person who loves a good story. I've got one for you.

After hitting $5M ARR in 3 years, with 0 external funding and $1M+ in profit in 2020, we decided to launch a challenge: raise $20M ... in 2 weeks.

Not only that, but we documented the entire process publicly.

At the end, we got two offers: one for $20M and another one for $30M. We refused both.

The news exploded all over the internet. We 've got **1M+ views and 1,5K+ shares in 5 days.** Plus, our story was shared with millions of people via French national news channels (such as Le Figaro, BFM, France Inter).

But wait, why did we decline the offers - you might ask?

Because we want to change the definition of startup success. Put the spotlight on profitability and create products that our customers want.

Help the next generation of entrepreneurs to build profitable businesses with or without raising money from investors.

Now this is where we need your help. Our founder, Guillaume Moubeche, wants to share our story with your audience, so that we can inspire and help more entrepreneurs to succeed.

If you'd be up for it, of course...

What do you think ... would our story be a good fit for your work?

Let me know your thoughts.
Briana

PS: If you want to see the main takeaways from the process, feel free to look at the deck. + short overview of who we are.

Here the {{tiramisu}} tag is replaced by a personalized sentence for each person we reached out to. Why do we call it tiramisu? First, because I'm part Italian and tiramisu is the best dessert in the world. But more importantly, because this sentence should be sweet like tiramisu because tiramisu literally means "pull me up". And that's what you want your intro to do. You want to catch your reader's attention from the start!

In order to be featured on TV, we decided to go with a PR agency using the exact same framework. The reason why we went through a PR firm is that we needed the warm intros from a trusted source.

We got featured on 10s of different TV shows, radio, and press channels and generated millions of impressions from it.

So far, we've seen all the steps to go from not having money to getting started to build and scale a business doing $10,000,000+ in annual recurring revenue. But during this journey you'll have several options, as a founder, to sell your company or a part of it.

We often talk about total or partial "exit". In the next chapter, I want to detail all the questions you might have regarding that topic and also discuss numbers!

But before reading forward, I have something exciting for you! Scan the code and register for a secret giveaway.

Key learnings

- You can boost your brand and get more people to trust you by doing interviews with top industry leaders. By spending time with them asking questions, you get associated with their image and people will perceive you as an expert as well.
- Processes are key.
- If you want to get people from the top of the ladder on your podcast/interviews you need to start small and then keep leveling up.
- Communities die, families prosper.
- Your team will be the most important success factor of your company as you grow.
- The key source of talented people is actually the people you've already hired.
- Your team reflects your company culture. That's why they need to be 100% involved.
- Making people's lives easier is one of the most underrated skills in business.
- Transparency leads to trust. Don't beat around the bush, tell it like it is and people will see they can trust you.

E. T

Growing and scaling a company is a very difficult job overall. As we've detailed in the previous chapters, the road will be full of ups and downs.

You take a lot of risks and put tremendous effort to pull your company off the ground. Once you get to the stage where you're generating enough revenue, you will get to the point where you can sell your company for a life-changing amount of money.

The process of selling a company is not very well documented, so in this chapter, I'll detail how we managed to sell our side project, lempod, after growing it to $600,000 ARR and why lemlist is now valued at $150,000,000.

I especially want to answer the following questions:

- Why should you sell your SaaS company?
- Why should you not sell your SaaS company?
- How do you know the worth of your SaaS business?
- How do you find buyers for a SaaS product?
- What are the different stages to go through until the sale?
- What are the 4 things to avoid at all costs?

Why should you sell your SaaS company?

There are many reasons why you should sell your SaaS company but here are the most common ones:

1. You have an offer you can't say NO to
2. You feel like it's time for you to do something new
3. You are tired of the risk of building a company

For us, it was neither of the 3 above...With both lemlist and lempod growing at a 2-digit month-over-month growth rate, sometimes we felt really frustrated! So obviously not because of the growth rate.

We were not able to do all the things we wanted to do for each project, whether it was on the tech side or business side. It took us some time to accept the fact that there are only 24 hours in a day.

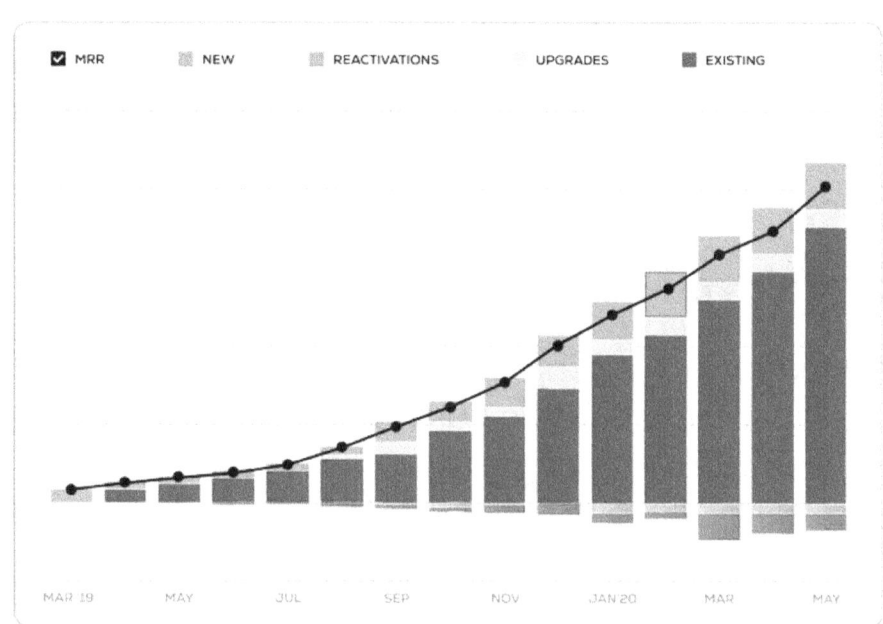

lempod's MRR growth from March 2019 to May 2020

lemlist being our first project, we've always considered it our baby. When we first started, we never thought that we could achieve the same 2-digit month-over-month growth after crossing the $1M ARR mark.

We thought that growing at such speed couldn't last forever, especially as a fully bootstrapped startup…but it did. Such a growth rate forces you to make tough decisions. It puts more pressure on both the support and tech teams…

With lemlist momentum being so extraordinary we decided to fully focus on its development and try to maintain the same growth rate, even though that meant selling another fast-growing SaaS: lempod.

Selling your SaaS company while it's growing fast is an important factor in the valuation of your product. But I'll go over that part later in this chapter!

You're probably wondering why we didn't hire more people to work on each project and keep them growing, and you'd be right...it's always important to know the areas you're good at, but also where you need to get better.

As a first-time SaaS founder, I've realized that hiring and scaling a team (at the time) was definitely not the part we excelled at. I needed to become better at it! Trying to scale 2 teams at the same time was not a route we wanted to take, so we thought that selling lempod and focusing on scaling the lemlist team seemed like a smarter choice.

Why shouldn't you sell your company?

When I got started with entrepreneurship I was sure that the road to success was all about growing a business and then making an exit.

Who doesn't like to brag about their new status as an "exit founder"? But after talking to many entrepreneurs, I realized 3 things:

1. A lot of people who sold their company regretted it afterward since they didn't think about what was coming next.
2. All exits are not equal. Sometimes after an exit, you have to stay working at your company for a certain amount of time before getting the full amount of money from the exit.
3. Running a profitable business is also a lot of fun. Going for an exit just because you have an opportunity is not always the smartest move both from a personal and financial standpoint.

The #1 reason why it's not always the smartest decision financially is because of compound effects.

Here is a post I made to explain what compound effect translates to:

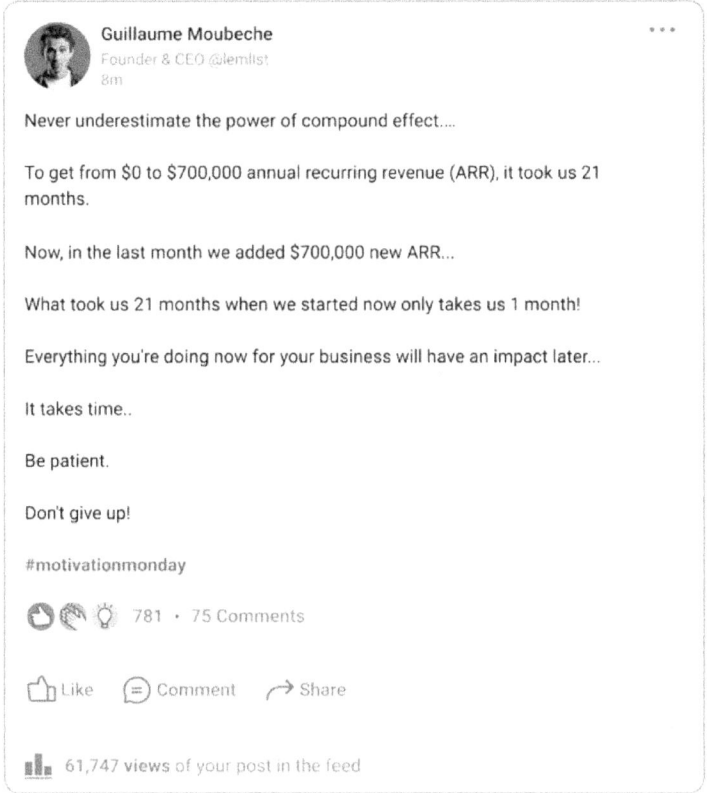

As your company grows you will see that all the things you've done compound. I will discuss how to value your company a bit later in this chapter, but you'll see that with this compounding effect, it is sometimes smart to wait a bit longer to exit your company in order to reach much higher multiples and profits.

How much is your SaaS business worth?

When you talk about SaaS valuation, it's really funny to see what people who never sold or bought a business have in mind.

I remember when someone asked in a group called "SaaS growth Hacks", how much a business doing approximately $27K MRR would sell for…

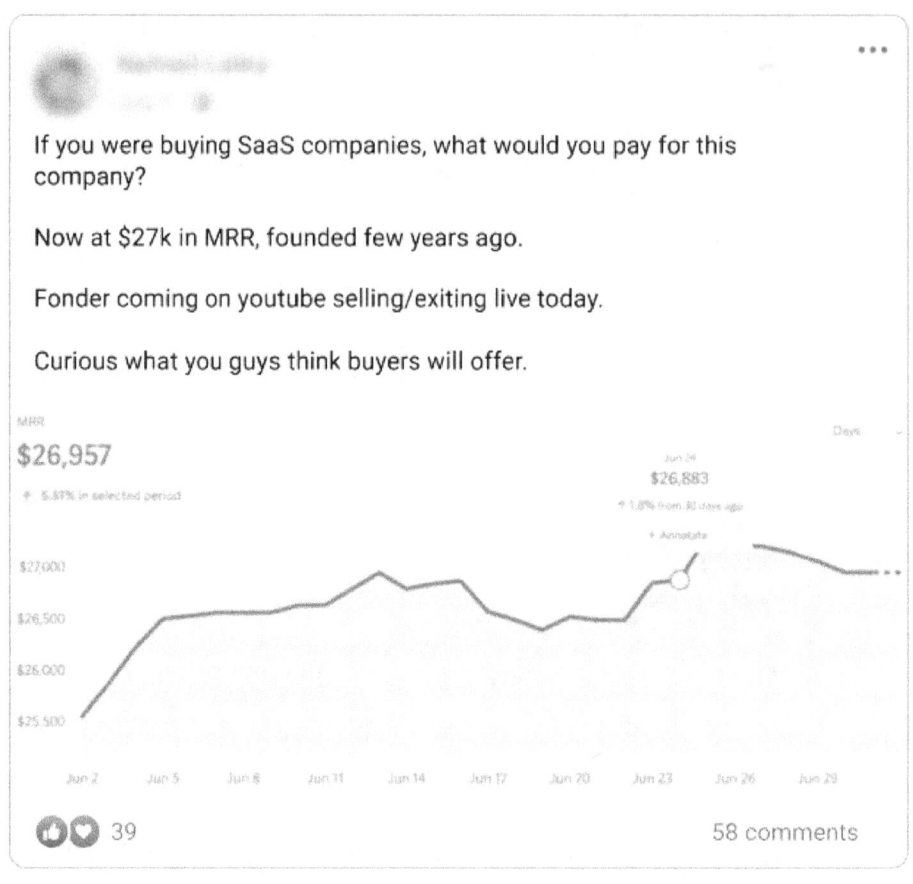

Someone asking for a SaaS valuation in SaaS Growth Hacks

To my surprise, people in the comments were valuing the business between 1.5x ARR up to 10x their ARR. It's funny to see that a lot of people gave valuation without having a clear overview of the business.

When you want to sell a business you will see that the most important parameters are the following:

- MRR (Monthly Recurring Revenue)
- ARR (Annual Recurring Revenue: calculated using MRR x 12)
- LTV (Lifetime value of your customers)
- CAC (Customer acquisition cost)
- Churn rate (how many customers are canceling their subscription each month)

- Growth Rate (how quickly you are growing each month)
- Cash burn rate (how much you are spending each month)
- Age of the business (When did you launch your business)
- Market (How big is the market? How competitive?)
- Risk (How likely something is to happen that could stop your business from growing and prospering?)
- Technology (what tech stack have you used? Do you have any technological edge?)
- Competitive advantage (What makes you unique? Do you have something no one else can copy?)

All these parameters will have an impact on your valuation, even though we've seen investors or potential buyers valuing businesses based on an ARR multiple.

For SaaS businesses, it generally makes sense as fixed costs[25] are known to be low. At least for a bootstrapped SaaS that seeks profitability rather than growth at all costs. Based on the different parameters mentioned above, SaaS businesses are usually sold between 2x to 4x the ARR if they are profitable and under $1,000,000 in ARR.

Once the business crosses the $1,000,000 in ARR the multiples can go to 4x to 7x and once the business crosses $10,000,000 in ARR this is where the multiples can skyrocket to 20x.

Again, this rule of thumb will not include some outliers where for example the competitive advantage or time to market could highly impact the valuation.

The most common misconception in business valuation comes from what is told in the media. Most people consider the valuation a startup gets during a fundraising process as the true valuation.

When you fundraise, the valuation of your company is not the present valuation, it's the future one. Let me explain. Let's say that you receive a funding offer of $20,000,000 at a $100,000,000 post-money valuation (20x ARR).

Most people would think that this "company valuation" would be equal to how much you could get if you were to sell the company… but that's not true.

This valuation means that with the $20,000,000 you would get during a funding round, the expected valuation you could get if you use that money the right way would be $100,000,000.

The issue here comes from the "expected" part. We see a lot of VC-backed startups that are raising money at crazy ARR multiples which means that they are forced to reach really high valuation later down the road in order to be able to exit their company. Which in most cases, never happens.

Now that you have a rough idea of what your company is worth, let's try to see the different exit options.

How to find buyers for a SaaS product?

Initially, when I was thinking about a company being acquired, I would always think about how bigger companies would acquire smaller ones because they would have a competitive edge (technology, brand, or market they're addressing).

However, I realized that these "strategic acquisitions" represent only a very small percentage of all acquisitions and mergers.

When selling a SaaS business, you have 4 different options:

1. Direct sale: when a buyer (company or private) comes to you (or the other way around) and asks to buy your company

2. Marketplace sale: there are tons of marketplaces where you can list your business (flippa, mircoacquire, etc.)

3. Auction sale: you can have a set of buyers willing to make an offer for your company (checkout "Deal or bust" from Nathan Latka)

4. Broker sale: you will go through a third party that will

help you find a buyer and that will get incentivized on the sale

A year and a half after starting lemlist I was asked to speak at various conferences across Europe (shameless brag). At some point, I ended up meeting Thomas Smale in Slovenia.

Meeting with David Henzel, the former CEO of MaxCDN (on the left) and Thomas Smale (on the right)

For those of you who don't know Thomas, he's the Founder of FE International, a SaaS M&A advisor. A SaaS M&A advisor usually has a big network of buyers and his role is to help you find the appropriate buyer for your SaaS.

The advantage of the SaaS M&A advisor is that they will do both the market research and the due diligence so when they introduce your SaaS to some potential buyers, they have a clear valuation on your business.

Their business model is pretty simple, they get a percentage of the total sale. That percentage can vary based on the person you work with and it often changes based on the deal size.

What I like about that business model is that as a business owner, you're not taking any risk upfront. If there's no buyer for your

SaaS, you won't have to pay.

There are other types of brokers that are taking an upfront fee and a much lower percentage on the sale, but since I've personally met Thomas and I had a lot of good feedback regarding his company, we decided to start working with him.

What are the different stages to go through until the sale?

This is where the fun begins! To complete the sale of your SaaS business, there are approximately 5 different steps.

1st step: Getting a valuation of your business

This phase is one of the most demanding for both founders and the broker. Essentially, FE International sent us a huge questionnaire for us to detail our business, the market, our competitive advantage VS competitors, potential growth opportunities, etc.

At the same time, we gave them access to both Profitwell and Stripe (our revenue tracking software) so they could see all our metrics in real-time (MRR, Growth rate, Churn, LTV, etc.). I also had a few calls with the FE team to answer questions regarding the business and the industry.

For about a month they worked on a sales prospectus that they were going to present to their list of buyers.

I was impressed by the level of detail they used in that prospectus. Every single detail of the business was clearly outlined, and the prospectus was about 30 pages long! Once we all agreed on what was stated in the prospectus, FE started the next phase!

2nd step: Going LIVE

There are two steps when going live. At first, FE shares their prospectus to some of their top buyers so they can have the best deals. Then, they decide to share the prospectus to their entire network.

Unfortunately for us, one week after we went live, the global lockdown started due to COVID…

The lockdown had a clear impact on the number of buyers and investments made worldwide as everyone was expecting a global crash of the financial markets.

Having so many companies with their stock valuation going down was a good opportunity for some potential SaaS buyers with cash to spend as buying undervalued stocks is a way to make some quick cash.

So due to the COVID crisis, we had to wait for about 2 months before actually meeting with some potential buyers.

3rd step: Meeting with potential buyers

This is the phase I liked the most. I was able to meet with potential buyers and exchange on different topics regarding lempod's growth and strategy.

lempod had really fast growth and a very low-cost structure. We were not spending any money on customer acquisition due to the virality of the product. This led most buyers to wonder why we wanted to sell.

On our end, our goal was to find a buyer who would be a good fit for the business. We wanted to find an entrepreneur (or team of entrepreneurs) who were willing to invest time and money to keep growing the business.

Because we also considered lempod as our baby, we wanted the buyers to be aligned with the vision as well.

After a week of meeting buyers, we found the right ones and received an offer quickly.

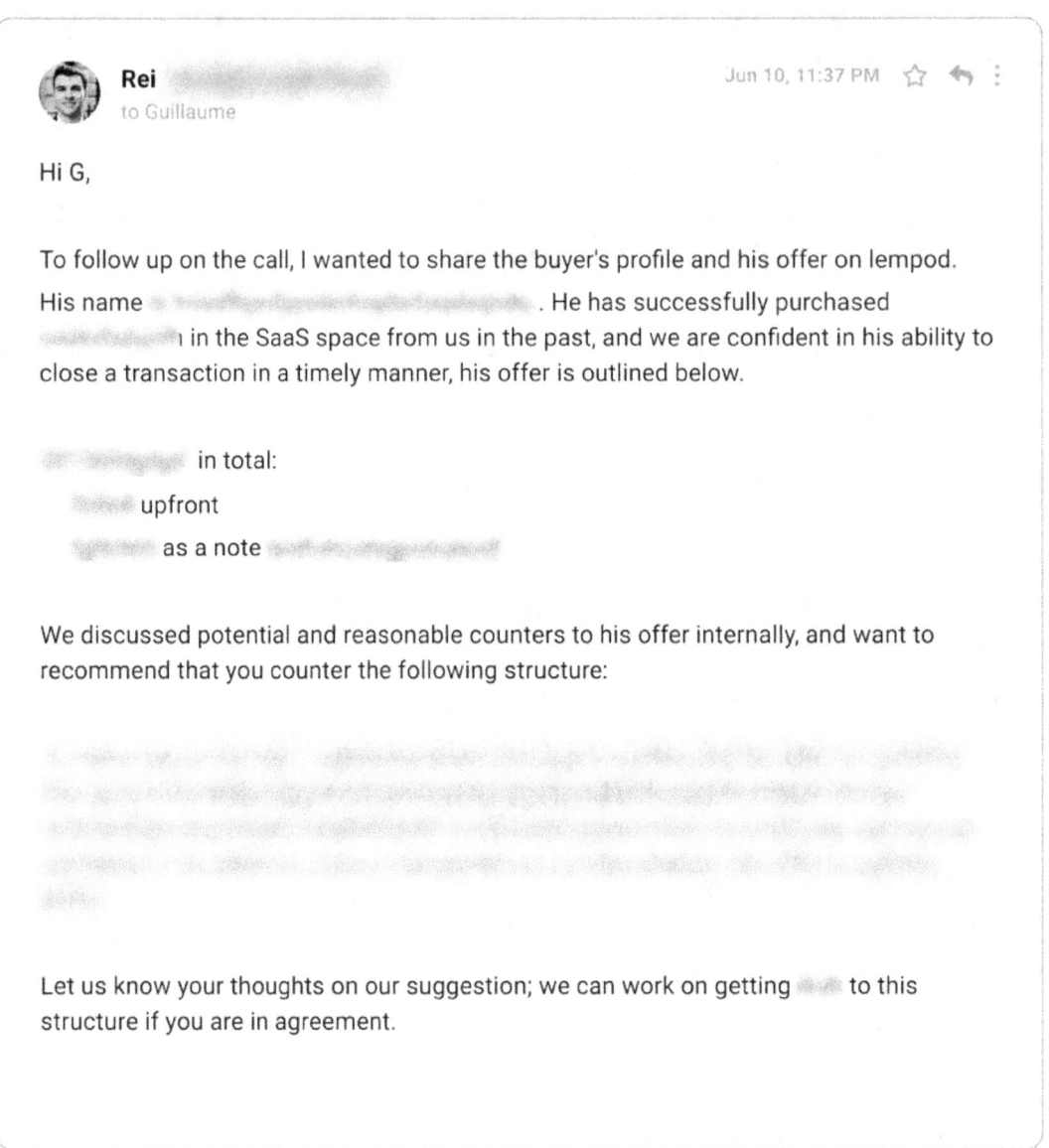

1st official offer we received to acquire lempod

4th step: Closing a deal

I was amazed by how quickly it went and was super excited about it. Before closing the deal, we had to negotiate some details first.

I've mentioned before how a business is valued based on many factors like MRR, Churn, LTV, etc. However, what I didn't mention is that the deal structure can vary. Indeed, most people think that when a business is sold, the founders are receiving a lot of cash and that's it.

Actually, you have many different ways to structure a deal. Usually, it will be a mix of cash at the time of the sale and what we call "earn-out". The earn-out is basically a period of time after the sale where you will receive more money.

People usually use earnout to involve the founders a bit more in the project. You can have an earn-out based on some milestones you'll have to reach to get more cash OR it can also be a percentage of the revenue.

What's nice about the way you structure your "earn-out" is that it allows both parties to mitigate the risk. The bigger the earn-out is, the less risk the buyer is taking as it means that the amount of cash upfront is usually smaller.

In the end, it's always a matter of negotiation and understanding what makes sense for both parties.

In our case, we won't be able to disclose the details of the deal we signed, but it was a mix of upfront cash and earn-out. The reason why we decided to add that earn-out part is that we were convinced back then that lempod would keep growing and hence we wanted to benefit from it.

5th step: Due diligence and transition

Once you agree with the buyers on the deal structure, you will sign a document that is called an LOI (Letter of Intent). This document is non-binding but shows that both parties have agreed to move to the next phase.

During this phase, the team will go through both technical due diligence[26] where they will check the codebase and business due diligence. The goal is to check that everything is in order.

For us it was super simple! We had 2 calls, one for the tech part and the other for the business side of things. Each lasted about 2 hours. We went through pretty much everything and answered all the questions.

Once done, you sign the official contract. In our case, this contract is called an APA which stands for Assets Purchase Agreement.

What's nice with it is that you're only selling your assets[27] (code base, website, customer base, etc.) and not the company itself.

This makes the process much smoother since it's a pain for international buyers to acquire the full company abroad. In other words, they are not familiar with the tax system or the legislation.

This part is one of the most important and even though FE works for you, I would always recommend you talk with your lawyers about such a contract. After a bit of back and forth, we were able to sign the contract within a week.

Once signed, it's now time to get paid! You will have to go through an escrow[28] process. The escrow is a third party that will ensure that the transition is done smoothly and that both parties are doing the things they have agreed on.

Essentially, the buyers will wire the money to the escrow so that when all the assets have been delivered to the buyers, the escrow will wire us the money.

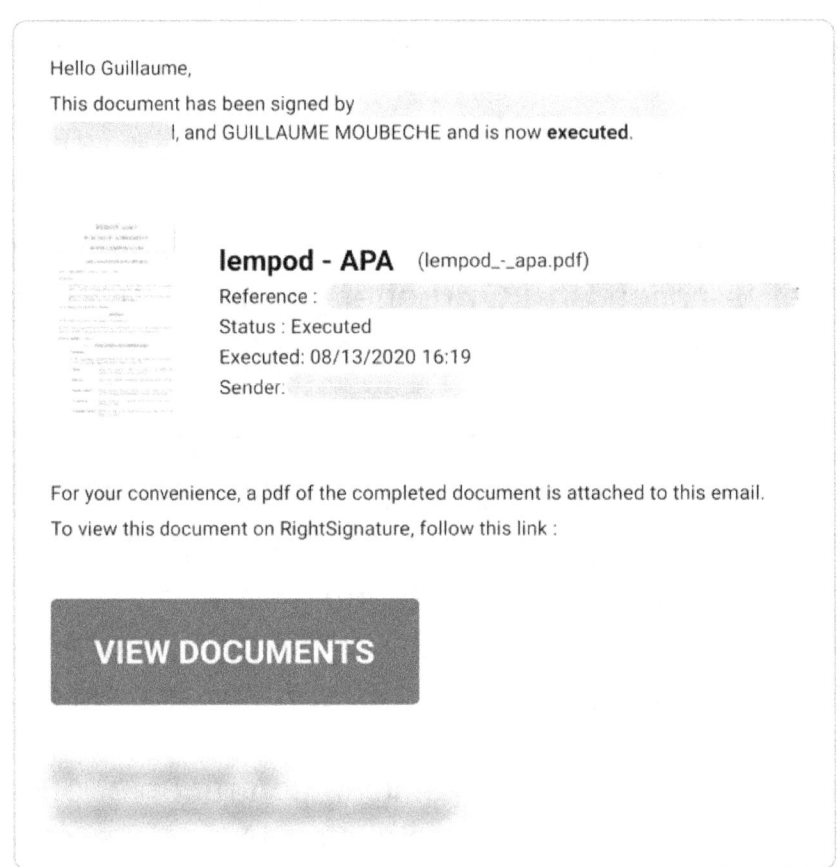

The confirmation email regarding the signed contract

We had planned the delivery of all assets (code base, domain transfer, Stripe account, tools used, etc.) to be completed within 5 days. In reality, it took 10.

Transferring the servers and the Stripe account including all customers was not something easy and it required quite some time from the dev team.

It can take a bit more time due to the technical aspect of it. We didn't want to impact too many users during the server migration so my two co-founders had to handle this over the weekend.

This phase was pretty smooth and while transferring all the assets, we also did some training to share all our growth secrets. We gave access to our entire growth workspace on Notion to the new team so they could re-use the same approaches that had the best ROI.

Once done, we finally received the money from the Escrow...leading to a huge champagne shower in Paris (just kidding).

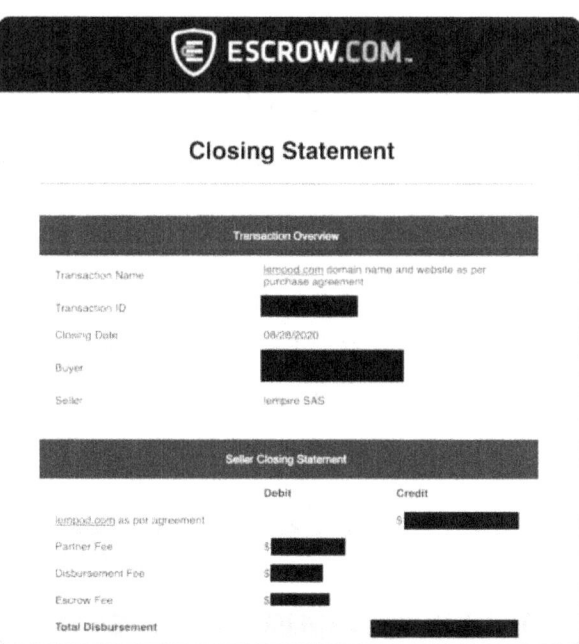

Payment confirmation from Escrow.com

The whole process took 6 months and it was a really fun experience with tons of lessons along the way.

4 things to avoid at all costs

We spotted a few things during the exit process that could have put us in a really bad spot...

After talking to dozens of SaaS founders who sold their companies, I realized that there were 4 things to really be careful about.

1. Due diligence on the buyer

The person or company that will acquire your company will be the one in charge of it afterward.

If you care a lot about your project and what you built, it's important that you trust the buyer and that you're aligned with what they want to do with the company.

Reach out to founders of companies they have acquired in the past and try to get as much info as possible on how it went during and after the sale. It will give you a general idea of what to expect.

2. Doing things on your own

Not all money is equal. And not all the money is worth the deal.

You think that the higher the price the better. That's absolutely NOT true. The terms of the deals are 10x more important than the actual money. Or at least they can really be a pain in the a**, so make sure to have really good lawyers on your side.

You should also ask entrepreneurs who went through the same process to check out the conditions of the deal, just to make sure that you are not signing something that you might regret later.

3. Staying in the company too long after the sale

Every entrepreneur I talked to that had to go through an earn-out period and had to stay at the company, regretted it. You go from being the CEO of your company to being the employee of someone who probably has different projects in mind for your company.

If you still want to do it make sure that the time frame is as short as possible. Talk to founders who have done it already and really weigh the pros and cons. In most cases, it's better to get less money but keep your freedom.

4. Not having a plan for what's coming next

We sold lempod so we could focus 100% on lemlist. We were lucky to have a plan and that forced us to be super cautious about the terms of the contract. We negotiated an earn-out without having to stay at the company.

For us, it was the best scenario. We would get cash upfront on top of some monthly earnout while at the same time being 100% focused on lemlist.

From my experience, the people who are telling you that they sell their company so they can go sip a cocktail on the beach are lying to themselves. Once you sell you'll be happy for about 5 seconds and then you'll ask yourself "What the f*ck am I gonna do now?" That's why having a plan for after is crucial.

If you're at the stage of selling, you need to think this through. Having a plan will help you avoid the post-sale depression that some founders encounter. You will realize that the money you get is life-changing but most entrepreneurs don't start a business solely because of money.

In most cases, money is actually not even a motivation past a certain milestone. Because what matters the most is the impact your company can have. Whether it's in your life, your co-founders' lives, your employees' lives, or your customers' lives.

The $150M valuation

So far, I shared all the secret strategies that helped us to grow to $10M in Annual Recurring Revenue in just 3.5 years being fully bootstrapped. I also mention that lemlist is now valued at $150M. Mentioning this valuation means that a deal happened…

If you've been reading the book thus far, you know our journey. And you know that we started our company with only $1000. Since the start, we never took any loans, nor money from investors - we actually even said no to a $30M funding round…

We were profitable from day 1 and the only money we used for that growth was our customers' money.

We truly believe that profitability is the most sustainable way to grow a business and we want to stay that way: bootstrapped, but with less risk…

In this part, I want to explain what type of deal we did in order to have a valuation of $150m in just 3.5 years.

I will explain the following in more detail:

- The difference between Cash-out and fundraising?
- Why does valuation differ depending on the type of financial operation you do?
- What deal did we make and why?
- Why Expedition Growth Capital?
- What is it going to change on a day-to-day basis for lempire?

The difference between Cash-out VS fundraising?

If you've been watching any startup-related media, you've probably stumbled upon articles about fundraising. The more money - the better!

The fundraising process works this way: investors will inject money directly into your company in order to help it scale faster. Fundraising is always tied to cash injection in order to "fuel the growth".

Truth to be told, I never thought that the amount of money you raised was correlated to your growth rate…but that's another topic.

Before the money is injected into the company, you need to set a valuation. That valuation is set in a consortium between the founders and the investors. That valuation is divided into pre-money and post-money valuation. Let's take an example to make it simple:

If a company raised $20M at an $80M pre-money valuation the post-money valuation is equal to $100M. So the post-money valuation is equal to pre-money valuation + amount raised. However, I see more and more people think that because a company is worth $100M it means that their founders are (or will be) super-rich…

Truth be told, a lot of founders I personally know who raised tens of millions ended up with nothing.

Why? Because when you fundraise, the money goes to the company. Not to the founders. That's the main difference between fundraising and what we call "cash-out" or "secondary".

A cash-out or secondary operation means that instead of giving money to the company, the investors will actually purchase shares in the company from the founders directly. It means that the money will go to the founders and not to the company itself. As you can imagine, the fact that the money is going directly to the founders will also impact the valuation, which leads us to our second question.

Why does valuation differ depending on the type of financial operation you do?

When a company fundraises, the injection of money is there to fuel the growth. When setting the valuation, the investors will focus on how the money they inject can help the company grow its revenue faster.

However, when you're selling a company, acquirers will actually have a look at financial metrics, profitability, growth, etc. Exactly what we discussed in the chapter detailing the sale of lempod.

To make it simple, investors are always betting on the future of the company while potential acquirers focus more on the past.

These differences make sense and that's why the valuation you get during fundraising is never the valuation you'd get if you were to sell your company.

When you're doing some "cash-out" or "secondary" the money will get directly to the founders. However, because it's not a total sale of the company, the investors will focus both on the past and on the future.

Their goal is to pay a valuation that would be a little bit higher than the real market value but to make a bet that the company will be worth 10 times that valuation in 4 to 5 years.

It's a big risk for them because they essentially give money directly to the founders without having any control of the company…

To sum it up, the valuation of your company will work as follows:

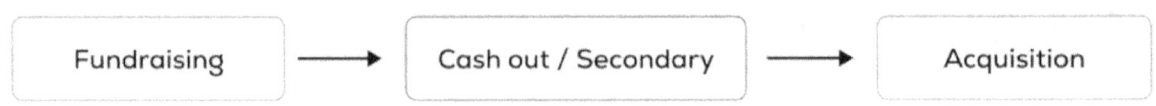

So now you're probably wondering…

What deal have we made exactly, and why?

At the beginning of this book, I stated that our company is now worth $150M. To set this valuation, my two co-founders and I made a deal to sell 20% of our shares for $30M.

The deal is simple. We, as founders, are taking $30M in cash, and in exchange Expedition Growth Capital will get 20% of the company and 1 seat on the board.

We keep full ownership of the company with 80% of the shares and 3 seats on the board.

You're probably wondering why we decided to make such a deal and also why not keep 100% of the company when you know that you're hyper growing and that your company will be worth 10 times more in the next few years…

It comes down to two parameters: pressure and risk. The bigger your company gets, the higher the valuation is, and the more pressure you have as a founder.

The decisions you make on a daily basis when you have 10 customers or when you have 10,000 customers do not have the same weight on your shoulders. The bigger the scale, the more impact, and weight each decision has.

On top of it, building and growing a company is always a risky process. As you grow, the risk of failure gets smaller (statistically) but on a personal level the risk level increases. You become the owner of a company that is valued at $100+ million without actually getting a single dollar in your bank account...which means that the higher the valuation of your business is, the more money you can potentially lose.

Being able to get $30M helped us own the most valuable asset a founder can have: peace of mind.

No matter what happens next, we will never have to worry about money ever again.

Some people will think that when you get such an amount of money, you can stop working entirely and retire. That's absolutely true.

My co-founders and I come from the middle class and we didn't grow up with a silver spoon in our mouth so we know how life-changing such an amount is. But to be honest, we didn't start this journey for the money. It might sound corny but we're truly passionate about our mission to help 1,000,000 entrepreneurs build and grow a profitable business.

We became much more ambitious with this money in our bank account and we're now able to take even more risks, follow our guts and solely focus on what we're passionate about.

To close this deal, we received many offers from different funds, but we didn't accept the one that was the most interesting financially, and here's why...

Why Expedition Growth Capital?

In the last 3.5 years, I've met a lot of investors from all over the world.

Documenting our entire journey and sharing our revenue milestones publicly leads to a pretty busy inbox.

☐ ☆	Will, Guillaume 2		Introduction - Hi Guillaume, Wanted to see whether you'd be interested in a brief in..
☐ ☆	Vincent, Guillaume 2		Intro - Hi Guillaume, Wanted to congratulate you on your impressive fundraise..
☐ ☆	Matt, Guillaume 2	Lemlist /	- Hi Guillaume, Nice to meet over email. Have heard good things about Lemlist ...
☐ ☆	Gennings, Will		- Hey Guillaume, hope you had a fantastic summer! My colle.
☐ ☆	Kimberly, Guillaume 5	Lemlist <>	- Hi Guillaume, Hope you're doing well and staying healthy! Tim (cc'd) and I wanted ..
☐ ☆	Haluk, Guillaume 5	Connecting with	- Hi Guillaume, I hope you don't mind the cold outreach! I'm an investor a.
☐ ☆	Jordan, Guillaume 3	Lemlist <>	- Hi Guillaume - I hope you're doing well! We haven't met before - my name is Is...
☐ ☆	Isabel, Guillaume 3	Lemlist //	- Hi Guillaume, Reaching out from ... we're a $630m bre...
☐ ☆	Magnus .. Guillaume 5	lemlist -	• Guillaume, I'm an investor at ..., and recently came across lemli.
☐ ☆	Shavon .. Guillaume 4		Interested in Lemlist - Hi Guillaume, I came across Lemlist while researching SMB
☐ ☆	Chris, Guillaume 3	Perfecting the outbound strategy	- Guillaume, I'm really interested
☐ ☆	Hanna, Guillaume 3		- Touching base in 2K21 - Hi Guillaume, Hope all is well! I know you had noted earlier...
☐ ☆	Katie, Guillaume 3	+ Lemlist Introduction	- Hi Guillaume, I hope this finds you well. I'm with ... a B2B software gro...
☐ ☆	mason, Guillaume 4	Lemlist //	Hi Guillaume, F... we're a $630m bre...

However, very few investors actually stand out with their cold emails (and I know a thing or two about that).

That was the case of the first email I received from Oliver, the managing partner at Expedition Growth Capital. They had prepared an in-depth presentation for lemlist. They knew and understood the competitive landscape very well and had spotted some interesting opportunities.

They had also done in-depth research, as they went to see some of our customers to ask for recommendations about lemlist. As you can see on the screenshot of one of their slides below. They went the extra mile to understand what our users thought about us. As an entrepreneur, you're always on the lookout for people going the extra mile, so I definitely wanted to meet with them.

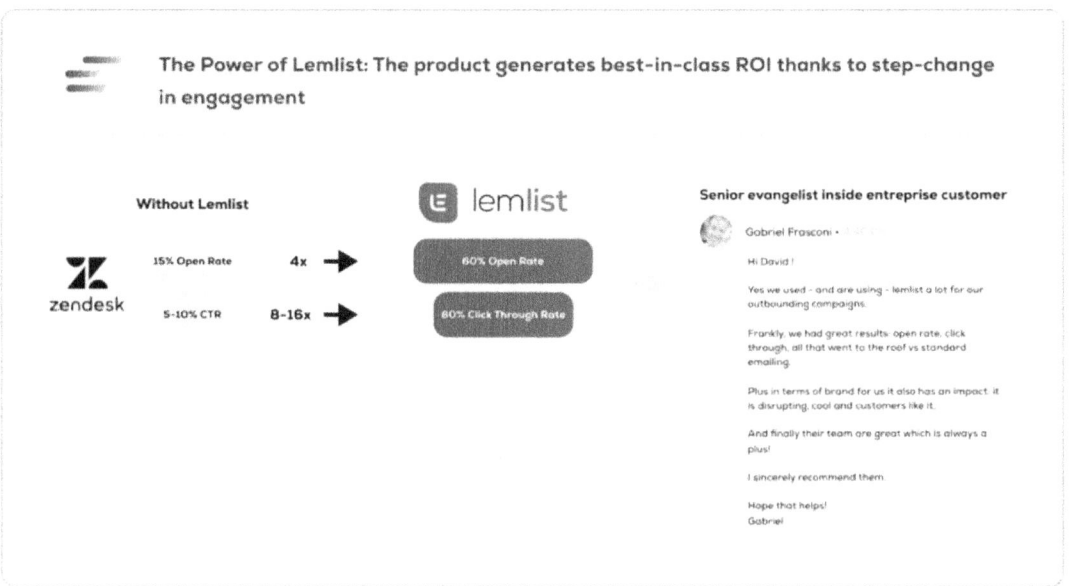

Being so user-centric even before knowing us was definitely something I had not seen in the past from any VCs.

From the start, they told us that they were happy to help founders sell some of their shares and do some cash out (meaning giving cash to the founder directly). It was really unexpected for me to hear this because most VCs I had a chat with in the past didn't want to do secondary at all (or a ridiculous percentage of the total fundraise).

For most VCs I've talked to, it's actually a red flag when a founder asks for too much cash-out. They think that if the founders don't have enough "skin in the game" they'll leave or won't be as involved as they used to be.

For Oliver, it was the opposite. He invests in profitable and bootstrapped businesses where he knows that the founders are not only driven by money.

I remember him telling me that he believed it was the best way for founders to be even more ambitious!

To him, the bigger a business gets the more weight on the founders' shoulders. Doing some cash out is the best way to relieve that weight from your shoulders.

I enjoyed the transparent communication from the start. No fluff, as well as the fact that they were really result-oriented. For the first time, I had people challenging our vision, asking tough questions.

In the end, what was difficult for us was to decide whether or not we wanted someone external to own shares. We didn't want to change the way we were working even though our company structure has always been extremely unconventional.

From the start to the end of the process Oliver was crystal clear. If we managed to grow a company to $10M in ARR in 3.5 years with only $1000 - he doesn't want to interfere in any way with the business operations and day-to-day life.

On top of it, he can help if we ask for it but for him, it was essential to give us as much freedom as we needed to keep running the business as we did...with a few changes....

What is going to change on a day-to-day basis?

As I mentioned above we now have one more partner at the table! This means that 2 main things will change:

1. We will start doing "board meetings".

Once every quarter we will do a meeting with Oliver and David in order to discuss both current results and future plans.

To me, that's really something I'm looking for because I realized that the more time we spent with Oliver and David talking about the business, the clearer our vision got. They always ask the right questions which push us to be sharper and it benefits the entire company.

2. We will have to do a monthly financial report.

I'm really excited about that part because we just hired a part-time CFO, Mathieu, who's handling all the financial reporting in order for us to be able to follow how our revenue is evolving based on our different segments of customers (which is something we were not doing in the past).

Both of these changes have a great impact on the business because they allow us to be challenged and also be more structured, all while keeping full control.

Key learnings

- Growing and scaling a company is a road full of ups and downs.
- Profitability is the most sustainable way to grow a business.
- The bigger your company gets, the higher the valuation is and the more pressure you have as a founder.
- Networking and building relationships can get you meetings with potential investors, acquirers, future employees, co-founders, etc.
- The bigger a business gets, the more weight on the founders' shoulders. Doing some cash out is the best way to relieve that weight from your shoulders.
- Not all money is equal. And not all money is worth the deal.